LISA
ENJOY!
CHEF DEZ
2024

Cooking Around
The World
with Chef Dez

ANOTHER GREAT
COOKBOOK FROM
CHEF, WRITER, & HOST:
CHEF DEZ

DEDICATION

To my dad, Bob.
For your love of cooking,
and the love you have given me
over the years.

CONTENTS

ACKNOWLEDGMENTS

I want to thank everyone who has attended my classes,
welcomed me into their homes & businesses,
attended my cooking shows, bought my books, travelled with me,
followed me on social media, and has been
a dedicated reader of my columns.

Without you… none of this would be a reality.
Thank you all so much.
I am so grateful.

SPREADS, DIPS, & SALSAS

Fire Roasted Corn & Black Bean Salsa

"Fantastic accompaniment at your next BBQ – great on grilled steak, chicken, and fish... or serve it as an appetizer with your favourite tortilla chips"

2 cobs sweet corn, husks removed
1 large red bell pepper, cut into large pieces
1 medium red onion, sliced thick
2 tablespoons canola oil
1/2 cup rinsed and drained canned black beans
1/4 cup oil packed sundried tomatoes, drained & finely chopped
1/4 cup firmly packed finely chopped fresh cilantro
2 garlic cloves, minced or crushed to a puree
Zest of 1 lime, finely chopped
Juice of 1 lime
1/2 teaspoon salt
1/4 teaspoon fresh cracked pepper

1. Preheat your grill for med-high heat, direct cooking over the charcoal/flame.
2. Toss the corn, red pepper, and onion with the canola oil to coat.
3. Grill until mostly charred. Let cool.
4. Cut the corn kernels off the cobs and chop the red pepper and onion into small pieces. Transfer all to a medium sized bowl.
5. Stir in the remaining ingredients and serve!

Makes approximately 4 cups

Honey Mustard Sauce

"So simple, and perfect with Crispy Pan-Fried Chicken Fingers. Makes almost 1 cup."

3/4 cup Mayonnaise
1.5 tablespoons yellow mustard
1.5 tablespoons liquid honey
1/2 teaspoon salt

1. Mix together and serve immediately or keep refrigerated for 5 to 7 days until needed.

Hummus in a Pressure Cooker - Makes approximately 2 cups

"Prepare hummus anytime without having to soak the chickpeas"

1 cup dry chickpeas
4 cups water
3 garlic cloves
1/4 cup tahini or smooth peanut butter
3 tablespoons fresh lemon juice
1 tablespoon extra-virgin olive oil
2-3 tablespoons reserved cooking liquid
1 teaspoon ground cumin
1/2 to 1 teaspoon salt

1. Add the chickpeas and water to the pressure cooker. Close and lock the lid in place and heat to build pressure. Turn down the heat and cook for 50-60 minutes and adjust the heat if necessary, to maintain pressure on high pressure (if steam is being released, lower the heat further).
2. Release the pressure following your manufacturer's recommendation. Remove the cooked chickpeas from the liquid and let cool. Remember to reserve 2 to 3 tablespoons of the residual cooking liquid.
3. While waiting for the chickpeas to cool, process the garlic in a food processor until finely minced.
4. To the food processor, add the cooled chickpeas, tahini or peanut butter, lemon juice, olive oil, chickpea liquid, cumin, and salt. Process until smooth and serve.

Kicked-Up Cocktail Sauce – makes approximately 3/4 cup

"Kind of like classic cocktail sauce for shrimp, but much better! Perfect with my Coconut Fried Shrimp"

1/2 cup apricot jam
4 teaspoons wholegrain mustard
4 teaspoons soy sauce
3 teaspoons prepared horseradish

1. Combine all ingredients together and serve at room temperature for dipping.

Red Onion Marmalade

"This is great on burgers, sandwiches, served with crackers & cheese, and many other applications. Makes approximately 2 cups."

1 tbsp canola oil
5 medium/small red onions, about 6.5 - 7 cups thinly sliced
3/4 teaspoon salt
1/2 cup brown sugar (not golden sugar)
1 cup red wine
1/2 cup balsamic vinegar

1. In a large pan on medium heat, add the oil and then the onions and salt. Stir to combine and cook, stirring occasionally, until the onions just start to brown on the pan a bit, approximately 20 minutes.
2. Stir in the brown sugar and allow the mixture to caramelize, stirring occasionally, approximately 15 minutes.
3. Stir in the red wine and the balsamic vinegar and continue to cook over medium heat until it reaches a thick syrupy consistency, stirring occasionally, approximately 20 minutes. Then turn off the heat and let cool in the pan until room temperature. As it cools the mixture will get thicker.
4. Serve immediately or store in the refrigerator for up to 1 week.

APPETIZERS

Broiled Italian Tomatoes

12 medium Roma tomatoes, room temperature
Salt & freshly cracked pepper
1/3 cup finely chopped fresh basil
Extra virgin olive oil
150g-200g grated parmiggiano reggiano

1. Slice the tomatoes lengthwise (from core to bottom) into halves. Place the 24 halves, cut side up on a baking sheet (line with parchment for easy clean up).
2. Season liberally with salt and fresh cracked pepper.
3. Distribute the amount of chopped basil evenly on the tomatoes.
4. Drizzle a small amount of olive oil on each tomato.
5. Distribute the cheese evenly on the tomatoes. *Tip – hold each tomato half over the cheese bowl to catch any cheese that falls off, and then return them to the baking sheet.
6. Broil under a hot preheated broiler for approximately 4 to 5 minutes until the cheese is just starting to brown.

Makes 24 halves

Bacon Wrapped Meatballs with Dipping Sauce

"Ground chuck (available from your local butcher) is the perfect meat for meatballs as it is screaming with beefy flavour – combine this with bacon and you couldn't ask for a better dish! Make sure you soak the toothpicks in water for a few hours to prevent them from burning."

2 pounds ground chuck
2 large eggs
1/2 cup fine breadcrumbs
1/4 cup finely minced onion
2 tablespoons finely minced garlic (about 6 garlic cloves)
2 teaspoons dried basil
2 teaspoons dried oregano
2 teaspoons salt
1 teaspoon pepper
20 thin strips of bacon
40 thick toothpicks, soaked in water, then drained

Dipping Sauce
2 cups strained canned tomatoes, or tomato sauce
1 cup blueberry jam
1/2 cup brown sugar
1/4 cup white vinegar
2.5 teaspoons salt
2 teaspoons Worcestershire sauce

1. Preheat your oven to 400 degrees Fahrenheit.
2. In a large bowl, combine the ground chuck, eggs, breadcrumbs, onion, garlic, basil, oregano, salt and pepper. Mix thoroughly and then roll into 40 meatballs – they should each be approximately 1 inch in size.
3. Cut the bacon slices in half. Wrap each meatball with a half slice of bacon and skewer each immediately with a toothpick to prevent them from becoming unwrapped. Place them on a parchment lined baking sheet.
4. Bake for approximately 20 minutes, or until the internal temperature reaches a minimum of 71 degrees Celsius or 160 degrees Fahrenheit.

Remove from the oven and let them rest on paper towels for about 5 minutes.

5. While the meatballs are cooking, combine the strained tomatoes, jam, brown sugar, vinegar, salt, and Worcestershire in a small pot over medium heat and cook until heated thoroughly, stirring frequently. Puree with a hand blender until smooth.
6. Serve immediately with the finished dipping sauce.

Makes 40 meatballs

Capocollo & Pear Antipasti

"A wonderful appetizer of contrasting flavours with a beautiful display on the plate"

2 pears, cored, quartered & sliced thin
2 tablespoons lemon juice
1 tablespoon water
250g mild capocollo, shaved
75g Gorgonzola cheese
3 tablespoons whipping cream
3/4 cup pecan halves, toasted

1. Toss the pear slices in mixture of lemon juice and water, to prevent oxidization.
2. Arrange the pear slices in circular designs on 4 small plates, with points towards the outside of the plates.
3. Divide and arrange the capocollo in the middle of the 4 pear displays.
4. Cut or break the Gorgonzola into pieces. Place with the cream in a stainless steel bowl. Place over a pot of simmering water and stir until the cheese has melted and combined with the cream. Remove from the heat and let stand 2 – 3 minutes to cool slightly and thicken.
5. Drizzle the Gorgonzola cream over the capocollo and pears. Garnish with the toasted pecans and serve immediately.

Makes 4 portions

Cajun Pork Tenderloin Bruschetta

"Alternatively, cook the pork in step #5 over charcoal, instead of in the oven, for a great smoky taste"

2 tablespoons salt dissolved in 2 cups water
1 pork tenderloin (approx. 400g)
2 tablespoons sweet smoked paprika
1 teaspoon ground dried oregano
1 teaspoon ground black pepper
1 teaspoon salt
1/2 teaspoon dried thyme
1/4 teaspoon cayenne pepper, or more if you like it hotter

1 baguette loaf
Extra virgin olive oil
3 garlic cloves, peeled and kept whole

3 large Roma tomatoes, diced small (approx. 2 cups)
1/4 cup finely chopped fresh cilantro
1 garlic clove, minced
1 teaspoon salt
1 teaspoon balsamic vinegar
1/2 teaspoon white sugar
A few grinds of black pepper

2 tablespoons salted butter
1 garlic clove, minced

1. Add the pork tenderloin to the brine of salt and water. Let sit refrigerated for a minimum of 1 hour.
2. Preheat oven to 450 degrees Fahrenheit.
3. Mix the paprika, oregano, 1 teaspoon pepper, 1 teaspoon salt, thyme, and cayenne together on a large plate and set aside.
4. Slice baguette on slight angle into 20 to 24 slices (approx. 1/2 inch thick). Lay them on a baking sheet and drizzle with some extra virgin olive oil. Bake in the preheated oven until mostly crisp, approximately

10 minutes. Once the bread slices have cooled to the touch, rub them with the 3 cloves of raw garlic. Set aside.

5. Reduce oven to 400 degrees Fahrenheit. Remove the tenderloin from the brine and pat dry with paper towels. Dredge the pork in the reserved spice mix (from step 3) until thoroughly coated. Place on a small baking pan and bake in the oven for 20 to 25 minutes, or until the internal temperature reaches 150 to 155 degrees Fahrenheit. Let rest a minimum of 5 minutes at room temperature.

6. In bowl, mix the diced tomatoes with the cilantro, 1 minced garlic clove, 1 teaspoon salt, balsamic vinegar, sugar, and the few grinds of black pepper. Set aside.

7. Slice the pork into thin slices (as thin as you can). Melt the butter with the 1 minced garlic clove and toss with the pork slices.

8. Assembly: distribute the pork slices evenly on the bread slices. Mix remaining pork juices into reserved tomato mixture. Top the tomato mixture evenly on the pork covered bread slices and serve immediately.

Makes 20 to 24 portions

Crispy Pan-Fried Chicken Fingers

"Actually, it's called shallow frying (less oil than pan frying or deep frying), but still crispy and delicious. Breast filets are the strips that come off the underside of chicken breasts and are usually available to purchase separately from the chicken breasts."

1/2 cup all-purpose flour
1.5 teaspoons salt
1 teaspoon baking powder
1 teaspoon garlic powder
1 teaspoon onion powder
3/4 teaspoon paprika or smoked paprika
1/2 teaspoon pepper
2 large eggs
2 tablespoons cold water
1.5 cups Corn Flake crumbs
16 chicken breast filets
1/2 cup canola oil
Extra salt for dusting
Serve with Honey Mustard Sauce (in the "Spreads, Dips & Salsas chapter)

1. On a large plate, toss together the following ingredients and set aside: flour, salt, baking powder, garlic powder, onion powder, paprika, and pepper.
2. In a medium mixing bowl, beat together the eggs and water and set aside.
3. Place the Corn Flake crumbs on another large plate and set aside.
4. Dredge all the chicken breast filets in the seasoned flour.
5. Then, working with 2 or 3 at a time, dip the filets into the egg mixture (called an 'egg wash') while draining each one a bit by running it up the side of the bowl before transferring to the crumbs (called the 'breading'). Coat liberally until completely coated with Corn Flake crumbs and then set aside on a tray. Repeat with all the filets.
6. Heat a 10" skillet (I prefer cast iron because it holds heat so well) over medium heat. Add the oil and heat the oil for about 3 to 4 minutes until hot. You can test the oil by partially dipping in one of the coated filets (you should hear it sizzling).

7. Working with 4 filets in the pan a t a time (4 batches total for the complete recipe 4 x 4 = 16 filets), pan fry on the first side for 4 minutes until golden brown and crispy. Flip them over and pan-fry for another 3 to 4 minutes until the second side is golden brown and the filets are cooked completely through. Internal temperature should be minimum 71 degrees Celsius or 165 degrees Fahrenheit.
8. Transfer the cooked filets to drain on paper towel, and immediately dust with the optional salt if desired. Let cool a bit before serving.

Makes 16 chicken fingers

Coconut Fried Shrimp

"Let's be honest: you can batter and deep fry almost anything and it would taste good, but these are fantastic – especially when served with my Kicked-Up Cocktail Sauce (in the Spreads, Dips and Salsas chapter of this book)."

Canola or vegetable oil for frying
1 cup all-purpose flour
1/2 cup sweetened shredded coconut
1 tablespoon sugar
2 teaspoons salt
2 teaspoons baking powder
2 teaspoons smoked paprika
1 cup beer
18 large prawns (16/20 size), deveined, tail-on
1.5 cups unsweetened shredded coconut
Fine sea salt or kosher salt, for dusting
1 recipe of Kicked-Up Cocktail Sauce (Spreads, Dips, and Salsas Chapter)

1. Preheat the oil in a deep pot (only filling no more than halfway) to a constant temperature of 350 degrees Fahrenheit.
2. In a medium mixing bowl combine the flour, sweetened coconut, sugar, salt, baking powder and paprika. Stir in the beer to make a smooth batter.
3. Pat the prawns dry with paper towel. Holding the prawns by the tail, coat in the batter all over, scrape excess batter on side of the bowl, and then dredge in the unsweetened coconut as a breading. Fry 3 or 4 shrimp at a time in the hot oil for approximately 2 to 3 minutes until golden brown, flipping them over in the oil halfway through the cooking time. Drain on clean paper towel with an immediate light dusting of salt as soon as they come out of the oil. Continue until all the prawns are cooked and serve immediately with the Kicked-Up Cocktail Sauce.

Makes six 3-prawn portions

Farinata

"This Italian thin savoury chickpea cake is typically cooked in a wood burning oven but can easily be done in your oven. Crispy on the outside and soft in the middle. Serve this as a starter or accompaniment to any Italian themed meal. I highly recommend using Italian Parmigiano Reggiano for the cheese."

1.5 cups chickpea flour
2 cups room temperature water
5 tablespoons extra virgin olive oil
1 tablespoon finely chopped fresh rosemary
2 teaspoons salt
2 teaspoons sugar
Freshly ground black pepper
1/4 cup grated parmesan cheese

1. Put the chickpea flour in a medium bowl and slowly whisk in the water until it is all combined and there are no lumps. Let stand uncovered at room temperature for at least 2 hours for the chickpea flour to fully absorb the water.
2. Preheat your oven to 500 degrees Fahrenheit. With a small spoon carefully skim and discard the foam that has formed on the top of the batter. Stir in 3 tablespoons of the oil, the rosemary, salt, sugar, and a few plentiful grinds of pepper.
3. Place an empty 10-inch cast iron frying pan in the preheated oven for 10 minutes.
4. Add the remaining 2 tablespoons of oil to the hot pan and carefully tilt and swirl the oil to coat the bottom and partially up the sides of the pan. Immediately pour the batter in the prepared pan and quickly top with the grated parmesan. Bake for approximately 20 minutes until set and browned.
5. Let rest in the pan for at least 5 minutes before removing and then cut into 16 wedges. Serve immediately or at room temperature.

Makes 16 small portions

Italian Style Wontons

"We made a version of these for guests at Limbert Mountain Farm years ago when I did cooking classes there"

125g provolone cheese, grated (about 1 cup grated)
3 tablespoons chopped fresh basil
4 tablespoons chopped fresh oregano
1/4 cup chopped walnuts
1/2 cup oil packed sundried tomatoes, drained & minced
1/2 cup olives, mixed variety, pitted and chopped fine
1 green onion, chopped
50 wonton wrappers

1. Preheat oven to 350 F (convection is better).
2. Combine all the ingredients together, except for the wonton wrappers.
3. For each wonton, place 1 wrapper on a flat surface. Spoon 1 teaspoon of this filling just below center of wrapper and shape the filling into a rectangle. Wet all 4 edges of the wonton wrapper with water. Fold bottom over filling, then tuck under filling. Fold the sides up to seal the left & right sides of the filling and roll forward to seal the wonton (should look like a little burrito). Place seam side down on a parchment covered baking sheet. Repeat with all remaining wonton wrappers and filling.
4. Bake for 10 to 12 minutes or until golden brown. Can also be deep fried instead if you prefer.

Makes approximately 3 cups of filling, and 50 filled wontons

Ginger Ale Tempura Batter

"Makes enough tempura batter for a whole variety of food – thin slices of sweet potato, bell peppers, whole prawns, etc. Substitute the ginger ale for a dark beer and you have a great batter coating for making fish for a classic fish & chips! An oil thermometer or a deep fryer with a thermostat is a must for this recipe."

1 cup all-purpose flour
1 cup cornstarch
1 tablespoon baking powder
2 teaspoons salt
1 large egg
1 – 355ml can of ginger ale
Canola oil for frying

1. Mix the flour, cornstarch, baking powder, and salt together. Whisk in the egg and the ginger ale until you get a smooth thick consistency. Keep the batter cold right up to the frying point.
2. In a large deep pot, add enough canola oil for about a 2 to 3 inch depth of oil. Heat the oil until you can maintain a consistent temperature of 350 to 375 degrees Fahrenheit.
3. Gently coat desired food and add to the hot oil one at a time, holding each piece in the oil until just starting to cook before letting it go. Cook until crispy and golden. Let drain on a rack and then serve with Tentsuyu dipping sauce.

Tentsuyu Dipping Sauce for Tempura

"Similar to what you get in restaurants. Provides a thin coating when dipping your tempura so this small quantity recipe goes a long way."

2 tablespoons soy sauce
2 tablespoons white wine
1 tablespoon finely grated fresh ginger
1 tablespoon fish sauce
1 tablespoon sugar
1 teaspoon liquid honey

1. Mix together until the sugar dissolves and serve.

South-Western Corn Fritters

"Less batter than a pancake, and lots of corn. If you don't have fresh corn, then use thawed frozen corn that has been patted dry really well, and then measure the 1.5 cups."

1.5 cups fresh corn kernels
1/4 cup small diced red bell pepper
1/2 jalapeno, minced (seeds & white membrane removed first)
2 teaspoons minced chives
2/3 cup all-purpose flour
4 teaspoons cornstarch
1 teaspoon salt
1/2 teaspoon pepper
2 large eggs, beaten
3 tablespoons milk
1/2 cup canola oil, for frying

Chipotle Sauce
1/2 cup mayonnaise
2 teaspoons liquid honey
1.5 teaspoons minced chipotle peppers (from a can)
1 teaspoon lime juice
1/4 teaspoon salt

1. Combine the corn kernels, bell pepper, jalapeno, and chives in a medium size mixing bowl. Add the flour, cornstarch, 1 teaspoon salt, pepper, eggs, and milk. Stir to combine to make a chunky batter.
2. In a separate small bowl, combine the mayonnaise, honey, chipotle, lime juice, and 1/4 teaspoon salt. Set aside.
3. Heat a 10" skillet (I prefer cast iron because it holds heat so well) over medium heat. Add the oil and heat the oil for about 5 minutes until hot. You can test the oil by putting a very small amount of the mixture (about 1/2 teaspoon) and you should hear it sizzling.
4. Take a standard size soup spoon and carefully put 4 heaping spoonfuls of the batter into the hot oil, in four spots. Fry until golden brown on the one side, before turning them over to brown the other side. Should

be approximately 3 minutes per side, but the golden-brown exterior is your goal. The time is just for approximation.

5. Transfer the four cooked fritters to drain on paper towel.
6. Repeat steps #4 and #5 to make 12 fritters total. Let cool slightly before serving with the chipotle sauce.

Makes 12 corn fritters (each approximately 2 to 3 inches in size)

Mediterranean Olive Tofu Crostini

"Crostini is Italian for fried bread and is traditionally served with a topping. I have combined crumbled medium firm tofu with kalamata olives and a handful of other Mediterranean ingredients and marinated them together. Topped on olive oil broiled Italian bread makes this a wonderful appetizer or brunch item. Makes 6 portions."

1 cup kalamata olives, pitted and chopped
115g (4oz) medium firm tofu, drained and crumbled
2 teaspoons anchovy paste
1 garlic clove, crushed to a paste
1 tablespoon chopped fresh oregano
1 tablespoon chopped fresh basil
1/4 teaspoon fresh cracked pepper
1 tablespoon extra virgin olive oil
2 teaspoons fresh lemon juice
1/2 teaspoon sugar
3 slices from a round crusty bread loaf, cut in half
1 to 2 tablespoons extra virgin olive oil

1. Mix the olives, tofu, anchovy, garlic, oregano, basil, pepper, 1 tbsp EVOO, lemon juice, and sugar in a bowl. Cover and let sit for a few hours or refrigerate overnight. If refrigerated, bring to room temperature before assembling/serving.
2. Brush the 1 to 2 tbsp of extra virgin olive oil on the bread slices and broil for 2 to 3 minutes until toasted.
3. Top the toasted bread slices with equal amounts of the tofu mixture and serve immediately.

Phyllo Pork Spring Rolls

"This is my version of a popular dish that we made regularly for different events at Limbert Mountain Farm in Agassiz, BC. I have many fond memories of this venue and the owners Claude & Trudie. Serve with your favourite Asian dipping sauce, or something as simple as plum sauce. Recipe note: sambal oelek is a hot chili paste found in the imported food aisle of your grocery store"

13 sheets of phyllo pastry
1-pound (454g) ground pork
2 tablespoons canola or vegetable oil
1 cup finely chopped onion
1 cup finely chopped celery
1 cup finely grated carrots
3 tablespoons minced ginger
3 tablespoons minced garlic
1 tablespoon fennel seeds, ground
1 teaspoon garam masala
1.5 to 2 teaspoons salt
1/2 teaspoon pepper
1 tablespoon oyster sauce
1 tsp sambal oelek, optional
3/4 cup butter, melted

1. Thaw package of phyllo pastry in refrigerator for 48 hours in order for it to thaw thoroughly with less chance of the sheets sticking together.
2. Preheat oven to 375 degrees Fahrenheit.
3. In a large pan over medium-high heat cook the pork, while breaking it up into small bits with a spoon, until browned and cooked through, approximately 10 minutes. Remove the pork with a slotted spoon and set aside.
4. In the same pan, over medium heat, add the oil, onion, celery, carrots, ginger, garlic, ground fennel seeds, garam masala, salt and pepper. Stir to combine, and cook while stirring occasionally, until the vegetables are soft, approximately 3 to 5 minutes.
5. Remove the pan from the heat and stir in the reserved cooked pork from step 1, along with the oyster sauce and sambal oelek.

6. Take one sheet of phyllo pastry with the long side facing you. With a pastry brush, butter the right half and fold the sheet in half (left part over buttered right part). Then butter the bottom half of this folded sheet and fold it in half once again (top part over buttered bottom part). Then make a vertical cut to cut this into 2 portions. Place 2 tablespoons of filling onto each of these 2 portions of prepared phyllo dough. Starting with the long side facing you, roll the filling into the dough burrito style (tucking in the sides as you go) while rolling away from you. Place these 2 completed rolls on a parchment lined baking sheet and brush with more butter. Repeat with the remaining 12 sheets of phyllo pastry.
7. Bake for 20 to 25 minutes until golden brown. Let cool slightly before serving.

Makes 26 rolls

Photo by Dale Klippenstein

SALADS

Coleslaw Vinaigrette Dressing

"A great alternative to high fat mayonnaise based coleslaw dressings. Mix with 5 cups of shredded cabbage or coleslaw mix."

1/4 cup white sugar
1/4 cup white vinegar
2 tablespoons canola oil
2 tablespoons grated onion
1 teaspoon yellow or Dijon mustard
1/2 teaspoon salt
1/2 teaspoon celery salt
1/4 teaspoon pepper

1. Mix together thoroughly and toss with 5 cups shredded cabbage or coleslaw mix.

Green Bean Salad

Recipe created by Katherine Desormeaux (Mrs. Chef Dez)
"A very simple salad for when fresh green beans are at the peak of the season"

6 cups cut green beans, cut diagonally in half, approx 2 inch pieces
1 red bell pepper, cut in similar size/shape as the beans
1/2 cup sliced red onion, cut in similar size/shape as the beans
Juice of 1 lemon
1/3 cup extra virgin olive oil
2 tablespoons sugar
1 teaspoon salt

1. Steam the green beans until cooked but still firm, approximately 2 minutes. Immediately plunge them in an ice-water bath to halt the cooking process. Once cold, drain thoroughly.
2. In a large bowl toss the green beans, red pepper and onion together.
3. In a small separate bowl, whisk together the lemon juice, oil, sugar, and salt. Pour over the green bean mixture and toss. Serve immediately.

Makes approximately 7 cups

Herbes de Provence Vinaigrette

"A basic vinaigrette focused on the herbes de Provence flavours"

1/2 cup extra virgin olive oil
1/2 cup white wine vinegar
1 garlic clove, crushed to a paste
1 tablespoon finely chopped fresh thyme
1 teaspoon finely chopped fresh basil
1 teaspoon finely chopped fresh rosemary
1/2 teaspoon dried marjoram leaves
1/2 teaspoon dried lavender flowers
1 teaspoon salt
1 teaspoon sugar
1/2 teaspoon fresh cracked pepper

1. Place all ingredients in a mixing bowl and whisk until combined ~ or ~ place all ingredients in a jar and shake until combined.
2. Refrigerate for a few hours if possible to let the flavours come together. Mix again and serve immediately before it has a chance to separate.

Makes just over 1 cup

Mexican Salads with Avocado Lime Vinaigrette

Vinaigrette (makes 2 cups)
1 large garlic clove
1 soft ripe avocado, pitted/peeled
1/2 cup fresh lime juice
1 tablespoon white sugar
2-3 teaspoons sambal oelek*
1 teaspoon ground cumin
1 teaspoon dry mustard
1 teaspoon salt
A few grinds of pepper
1 cup extra virgin olive oil

Salads
312g box of wash mixed organic greens
1 – 540ml can of black beans, rinsed & drained
1 medium zucchini, quartered lengthwise & sliced thin
Kernels removed from 2 ears of fresh corn
1 large red bell pepper, diced small

1. To make the vinaigrette: Process the garlic clove in a food processor until finely minced. Add all the other ingredients except for the oil and process smooth. With the processor running, drizzle in the oil slowly to complete the vinaigrette. Set aside.
2. Assemble the salad ingredients on the plates in the order listed above. Top each of the 10 salads with 3 tbsp of vinaigrette each and serve.

Makes 10 small salads

*Sambal oelek is an Indonesian chili sauce or paste typically made from a mixture of a variety of chili peppers. One can usually find it down the imported (or Asian) food aisle of major grocery stores.

Pesto Primavera Pasta Salad

"Use the Parsley Pesto Recipe found in the Sauces Chapter for this salad"

340g dry pasta shapes – penne, fusilli, shells, etc.
1 raw corn on the cob, kernels removed
2 cups broccoli cut into small fleurettes, steamed, chilled
1 cup grape tomatoes, quartered
1/2 cup sliced oil packed sundried tomatoes, drained
1 cup small diced mozzarella cheese
1 cup Parsley Pesto (recipe in the "Sauces" Chapter of this book)
1/4 cup grated parmesan cheese
Salt & pepper
1/2 cup slivered almonds, toasted, for garnish

1. Cooked the pasta until desired doneness. Rinse with cold water until thoroughly chilled. Drain well and add to a large bowl.
2. Add the following ingredients to the pasta and gently mix well to combine: corn kernels, broccoli, grape tomatoes, sundried tomatoes, diced mozzarella, parsley pesto, and the parmesan. Season to taste with salt and pepper once combined.
3. Serve with the toasted almonds on top as a garnish.

Makes approximately 10 cups

Sunomono Salad

"A refreshing starter to any Japanese themed meal"

Marinade
1 cup rice wine vinegar
1 cup water
4 tablespoons sugar
1 teaspoon salt

4 – 50g bundles of vermicelli noodles (200g total)
1/2 carrot, thinly sliced into sticks (julienne)
1/2 cucumber, halved and sliced thinly
1/2 lemon, sliced thin and each slice cut into 6ths
2 green onions, sliced thin on an angle
Cooked small shrimp, optional
Sesame seeds as garnish, optional

1. Heat the marinade to dissolve the sugar. Transfer to a bowl to cool completely in the refrigerator.
2. Boil 6 cups of water. Take off the heat and add the noodles. Let stand off the heat until tender, about 3 to 4 minutes. Drain thoroughly and transfer the cooked noodles to the cold reserved marinade from step 1. Let soak in the refrigerator for at least 1/2 hour.
3. Transfer the noodles and marinade equally into 6 small bowls.
4. Garnish equally with remaining ingredients.

Makes 6 portions

SAUCES

Béchamel Sauce

"One of the main French mother sauces; otherwise called a white sauce. Add cheddar cheese for cheese sauce for the perfect Mac & Cheese. Add gruyere and parmesan cheeses to make a mornay sauce – perfect for eggs, veggies, fish, or poultry."

2 tbsp butter
2 tbsp flour
1.5 to 2 cups milk
Pinch of ground nutmeg
Salt and ground white pepper to season

1. Melt the butter in a pot over medium low heat.
2. Stir in the flour and cook for a few minutes while stirring. Do not brown.
3. Slowly whisk in the 1.5 cups of milk (a little at a time at first), until all the milk is thoroughly combined with no lumps.
4. Season with nutmeg, salt, and white pepper.
5. Bring to a full boil while stirring frequently to fully thicken the sauce. Add more milk to thin it out if necessary.
6. Re-season to taste and serve.

Makes about 1.5 to 2 cups

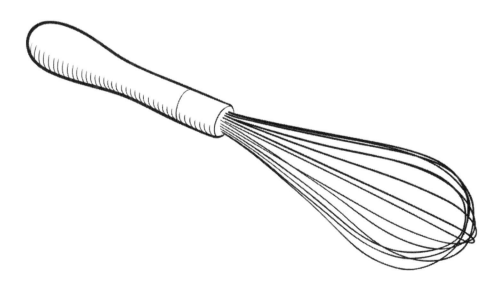

Blueberry BBQ Sauce

"A fantastic grilling sauce made from fresh or frozen blueberries. Tastes great on chicken, pork or beef!"

3 cups blueberries, fresh or thawed from frozen
3 garlic cloves, minced or pressed
1/4 cup dark brown sugar
1/4 cup minced onion
1/4 cup ketchup
1/4 cup white vinegar
1/4 cup molasses
2 teaspoons salt
1/2 teaspoon pepper

1. Add all ingredients to a medium heavy bottomed pot.
2. Turn heat to medium and bring to a boil while mashing the blueberries with a potato masher.
3. Once boiling, turn heat to low and simmer uncovered for 5 minutes.
4. Transfer to a blender and puree smooth. Most blenders can handle hot liquids but if you are unsure if yours can or not, let the sauce cool first before pureeing. Always be careful when handling hot liquids – make sure the lid of your blender is on tight and to be safe hold the lid down with a towel or oven mitt to protect your hand.

Makes approximately 2.5 cups

Chow Chow Sauce

"Chow chow is another name for North American pickled relish, so I thought this would be a catchy name for the sauce to define its main ingredient of relish. This is great served with spice-rubbed grilled meats."

1/2 cup sweet pickle relish
1/4 cup yellow mustard

3 tablespoons mayonnaise
2 tablespoons liquid honey
1 tablespoon apple cider vinegar
2 teaspoons Worcestershire sauce
1/4 teaspoon salt

1. Mix all ingredients together thoroughly. Keep refrigerated if not using right away, otherwise serve at room temperature on a variety of cuts of grilled rubbed beef or pork.

Makes just over 1 cup

No–Cook BBQ Sauce

"Great for the kids to make – no cooking required, just measuring and mixing"

1/2 cup ketchup
1 tablespoon molasses
1 teaspoon white vinegar
1/2 teaspoon chili powder
1/2 teaspoon Worcestershire sauce
1/2 teaspoon hot sauce **or** 2 drops Tabasco sauce
Pinch of salt
Sprinkle of cinnamon
Couple drops of liquid smoke, optional

1. Mix together and keep refrigerated.

Makes approximately 2/3 cup

Parsley Pesto

"Pesto is traditionally made with basil, but parsley is more readily available and works extremely well in this recipe! Makes approximately 1.5 cups."

2/3 cup roasted, salted cashews
1/2 cup extra virgin olive oil
1/2 cup grated Parmesan cheese
2 large garlic cloves, peeled
juice of a 1/2 lemon
1/2 teaspoon salt
1/2 teaspoon fresh cracked pepper
1 bunch fresh curly leaf parsley, large stems removed

1. In a food processor, grind the cashews on high speed for approximately 15 seconds.
2. Continue to process on high speed while slowly adding ¼ cup of the olive oil through the top opening, and then process for another 30 seconds until mixture is almost completely smooth and liquid.
3. Turn off the processor. Add the cheese, garlic, lemon juice, salt, and pepper. Turn the processor back on and process on high speed while feeding the parsley through the top opening. When all of the parsley has been added, continue to process on high speed while slowly adding the remaining ¼ cup of olive oil.
4. Turn off the processor, scrape down the sides, and process for another 10 to 15 seconds.
5. Toss with hot freshly cooked pasta of your choice or use in a variety of applications such as a pizza or bruschetta topping."

Red Onion Gravy

"A simple gravy traditionally served on Toad In The Hole (see the pork chapter in this book), but also great on any pork or beef dish. Makes approximately 2 cups."

3 tablespoons butter, separated
1.5 cups thinly sliced red onion (1 medium/large red onion)
1/2 teaspoon salt

2 tablespoons all-purpose flour
2 cups beef broth
1/2 teaspoon sugar

1. Heat a pan over medium heat for 1 minute.
2. Melt 2 tablespoons of the butter until foamy. Stir in the onion and salt. Cook for 10 minutes, stirring occasionally, until the onion slices are soft and they begin to caramelize.
3. Stir in the remaining 1 tablespoon of butter and the flour. Cook for 2 minutes stirring frequently.
4. Gradually stir the beef broth until fully combined. Add the sugar. Bring to a boil over high heat, and then turn the heat down to medium-high and continue to cook, stirring frequently, until desired consistency is reached, about 2 minutes.

Velouté Sauce

"Make this with chicken stock, fish stock, or veal stock — depending on what the application is. Makes 1.5 to 2 cups."

2 tablespoons butter
2 tabelspoons flour
1.5 to 2 cups stock (chicken, fish or veal)
Salt and ground white pepper to season

1. Melt the butter in a pot over medium low heat.
2. Stir in the flour and cook for a few minutes while stirring. Do not brown.
3. Slowly whisk in the 1.5 cups of stock (a little at a time at first), until all the stock is thoroughly combined with no lumps.
4. Season with salt and white pepper.
5. Bring to a full boil while stirring frequently to fully thicken the sauce. Add more stock to thin it out if necessary.
6. Re-season to taste and serve.

Soups & Stews

French Onion Soup

"Using a combination of beef broth and red wine, along with the caramelized onions makes this soup very robust in flavour. How much salt you add at the end to season will depend upon how much salt is in your beef broth."

3 tablespoons butter
5 medium onions (about 1100g), halved and sliced thin (about 8 cups sliced)
2 tablespoons brown sugar (not golden sugar)
1/2 teaspoon salt
1 baguette
1 cup full bodied red wine
6.5 cups beef broth
2 bay leaves
2 large sprigs fresh thyme
Salt & pepper
300g gruyere cheese, grated

1. Over medium-high heat, melt the butter in a large pot until foaming.
2. Add the onions, brown sugar, salt and turn the heat to medium. Cook, stirring occasionally, for 30 to 45 minutes until the onions have reduced and caramelized, and they start to brown the bottom of the pot.
3. While the onions are cooking, preheat the oven to 450 degrees Fahrenheit. Slice the baguette into 12 slices: 1/2 inch thick on a 45 degree angle (enough for 2 slices per serving) and place them on a baking sheet. Toast in the oven for 5 minutes and set aside.
4. Once the onions have caramelized, add the wine, broth, bay leaves, and thyme to the pot. Bring to a boil over high heat and then reduce the heat to simmer, uncovered, for 30 minutes to concentrate the flavours. Season to taste with salt & pepper.
5. Remove and discard the bay leaves and thyme sprigs. Ladle the soup into 6 "oven-proof" bowls. Top each bowl with 2 toasted baguette slices and an equal amount of grated cheese. Broil in the oven until the cheese is melted and golden. Serve immediately.

Makes 6 portions

Greek Lemon Soup (Avgolemono)

"A very authentic version of this classic Greek soup. The name of this soup is Avgolemono from the ingredients eggs (avgo) and lemon juice (lemoni)."

8 cups chicken broth
1 cup long grain rice
1/2 teaspoon salt
4 large eggs
3/4 cup fresh lemon juice (approximately 4-5 large lemons)
1 teaspoon sugar
Reserved zest from lemons
Chopped fresh parsley

1. In a large saucepan or pot over high heat, bring the chicken broth to a boil.
2. Stir in the rice and the salt. Cover, reduce the heat to low and simmer for 20 minutes.
3. Separate the egg yolks from the egg whites.
4. About 5 minutes before the rice is done cooking in the broth, beat the yolks together in a small bowl, while in a large separate bowl whisk the egg whites until stiff peaks have formed. Slowly beat the mixed yolks into the whites. Then gradually beat the lemon juice into this egg mixture.
5. Gradually add 2 cups of the hot broth/rice mixture into the egg/juice mixture while whisking continuously. If the hot stock is added too fast, the eggs will curdle.
6. Once the 2 cups of broth have been added, stir the egg mixture into the large saucepan with the remaining broth/rice. Season with 1 teaspoon of sugar and serve immediately, garnished with the lemon zest and a small amount of chopped parsley.

Makes approximately 10.5 cups

Slow Cooker Thai Squash Soup

1 medium onion, chopped
2 – 3 large garlic cloves, chopped
2 tablespoons minced fresh ginger
3 – 4 teaspoons red Thai curry paste
3 tablespoons sugar
1 tablespoon salt
10 cups of 1/2-inch cubed, peeled, seeded butternut squash
2 cups chicken stock
1 – 400ml can of coconut milk
Juice of 1 lime
Salt & pepper to season
Optional garnish: Toasted grated sweet coconut, toasted pumpkin seeds, fresh cilantro

1. Add the onion, garlic, ginger, curry paste, sugar, salt, kabocha, butternut, chicken stock, and coconut milk (with the thick coconut cream on the surface of the canned milk) to a slow cooker. Stir thoroughly to combine.
2. Cook on low setting for 7 to 9 hours until the squash is tender.
3. Puree with a hand submersion blender (or food processor, or blender) until the texture is very smooth. Stir in the fresh lime juice and season to taste with salt and pepper, if desired. If the consistency is too thick add some more chicken stock.
4. Garnish each bowl and serve immediately.

Makes approximately 9 cups

Prawn Bisque – serves 4

2 tablespoons butter
1 celery stalk, sliced
1 carrot, sliced
4 – 6 garlic cloves, chopped
1 small onion, chopped
680g black tiger prawns with shells, peeled, & shells reserved
Salt & pepper
1/2 cup white wine
2 bay leaves
2 teaspoons dried tarragon
----
2 teaspoons canola oil
1 large shallot, minced
1.5 cups fish stock
1/4 cup brandy
3 tablespoons tomato paste
1 cup whipping cream
1/2 teaspoon salt
1/2 teaspoon pepper
Chopped parsley, for garnish

1. Place the butter in a large pan over medium heat and when butter starts to foam, add the celery, carrot, garlic, onion, and the shells from the prawns (reserve the prawn meat for later). Season with salt & pepper and cook for 2 to 3 minutes until the vegetables have softened a bit. Add the wine, bay leaves and tarragon and bring to a boil. Cover & simmer for 10 to 15 minutes to bring out the flavour of the prawn shells. Strain and reserve the liquid in a separate container (discard the solids).
2. Put the pan back on medium heat; add the canola oil and sauté the shallot for 1 minute.
3. Add 1/4 (one quarter) cup of the fish stock to deglaze the pan. Carefully add the brandy and carefully ignite with a long match/lighter. Flambé until the flames subside.
4. Stir in the tomato paste, and then add the remaining 1.25 cups of fish stock, the whipping cream, 1/2 tsp salt, 1/2 tsp pepper, and the reserved liquid from step 1.

5. Add the prawn meat (cut in small pieces if desired) and bring to a boil while stirring until the prawns are just cooked. Re- season with more salt and pepper if necessary. Garnish with chopped parsley & serve immediately.

Zuppa Toscana – makes 9 cups

"The name translates to 'Tuscan Soup' and this is my version of the one you find at the Olive Garden Restaurant. This broth soup is only slightly creamy, so it is light but yet filling at the same time because of the potatoes and sausage. Lots of fresh kale for nutrition! I like to use russet potatoes as they fall apart more when cooked than red-skinned potatoes."

500g (or 1 pound) mild Italian Sausages
2 teaspoons fennel seed
1 teaspoon dried basil
1/2 teaspoon dried red pepper flakes
2 large potatoes, unpeeled, scrubbed
6 cups chicken broth
3/4 cup whipping cream
4 cups chopped fresh kale
1.5 teaspoons salt
1/2 teaspoon pepper
2 teaspoons white sugar
2 teaspoons fresh lemon juice

1. Squeeze the sausage meat out of the casings and add to a soup pot. Add the fennel seed, basil, and red pepper flakes. Turn heat to medium and cook, while breaking the sausage apart with a spoon, until the sausage is fully cooked, approximately 8 to 10 minutes. Drain this mixture in a fine wire strainer to discard the fat. Set aside.
2. Cut the unpeeled potatoes into quarters (lengthwise) and then slice into 1/4-inch pieces. Set aside.
3. To the pot add the chicken broth/stock, whipping cream, potatoes, kale, salt, pepper, and the reserved cooked sausage pieces from step one. Bring to a simmer over medium heat, and then reduce the heat to maintain a simmer uncovered for approximately 20 to 30 minutes until the potato pieces are tender.
4. Turn off the heat and finish with the sugar and lemon juice. Serve immediately.

Ramen in a Hurry

"My version of Ramen. Tasty and beautifully displayed in a fraction of the time of a traditional Ramen recipe. Plus, I do a crispy fried egg, instead of the common soft-boiled egg."

4 cups beef broth
2 garlic cloves, minced
1 tablespoon grated or minced ginger
1 to 2 tablespoons soy sauce
1 tablespoon rice vinegar
1 tablespoon sambal oelek*
2 – 100g packs of noodles (discard the seasoning packets)
2 tablespoons canola oil
8 to 10 thin slices pork tenderloin
2 large eggs
3/4 cup bean sprouts
2 green onions, thinly sliced at a 45-degree angle
1 small sweet red pepper, thinly sliced into rings
Nori, cut into a handful of small strips

1. In a medium pot, add the broth, garlic, ginger, soy sauce, rice vinegar, and sambal oelek. Bring to a boil over high heat, and then reduce the heat to simmer uncovered for 5 minutes.
2. After the 5 minutes of simmering, bring to a boil by increasing the heat and add the noodles. Cook for 3 minutes, or until desired doneness.
3. Meanwhile, heat a medium pan over medium/high heat until hot. Add the oil to the pan and fry the pork slices until cooked and crispy. Remove the pork from the pan (leaving the residual oil in the pan) and set aside.
4. As soon as the pork comes out of the pan, crack the 2 eggs into the pan and fry without flipping them. Once they are half set, poke the yolk and continue to cook until the bottoms of the eggs are crispy. Remove the eggs from the pan and set aside.
5. Divide the noodles and broth equally between 2 large serving bowls. Top with the crispy pork slices, crispy eggs, bean sprouts, green onions, red pepper, and nori. Serve immediately.

Makes 2 large portions

*Sambal Oelek is an Indonesian chili sauce or paste typically made from a mixture of a variety of chili peppers. One can usually find it down the imported (or Asian) food aisle of major grocery stores.

Broth Based Soup from Scratch – Customizable!

"This is a rough guide to get you pointed in the right direction when you want to make a broth based soup from scratch and you don't know where to begin. Measurements of ingredients (amounts) are up to you. Remember: the more you practice, the better you get!"

A small amount of cooking oil (like canola, vegetable, grape seed, etc)
Mirepoix: 2-parts Onion, 1-part Carrot, 1-part Celery – chopped as desired
A small amount of chopped Garlic
Small amount of Salt & Pepper
Herbs (fresh or dried – See Step #1 to know when to add to the pot)
Flavouring Ingredients: added vegetables, meats, hot peppers, etc.
Complimenting broth/liquid of your choice
Added filler ingredients: pasta, potatoes, grains (barley, rice, etc)
Seasoning to finish: Salt, Pepper, possibly a small amount of sugar if acidic ingredients (like tomatoes for example) are used.
Optional added thickener: like dissolved cornstarch
Garnish

1. Heat a pot slightly over medium heat. Add the oil, followed by the mirepoix and then the garlic and salt & pepper. If you are using dry herbs, or any woody fresh herbs that need cooking (like rosemary for example), add them now. Fresh delicate herbs should be added just before the soup is finished. Stir to combine. Cover and let sweat for a few minutes, stirring occasionally, until the vegetables are soft.
2. Add your flavouring ingredients and cook a couple minutes more. If you are using meat as one of your flavouring ingredients, follow this simple rule: Raw meats cooked first in the pot before the mirepoix and set aside; Cooked meats to be added with the broth, or after the filler ingredients (if used) are cooked.
3. Add your choice of broth and bring to a boil over higher heat.
4. If using filler ingredients, add them now and cook until these until tender. Keep in mind these ingredients will absorb some of the broth/liquid, and expand, so don't add too much.
5. Taste and season as necessary. If you choose to use cornstarch to make your soup thicker (less liquidy) add a small amount of cornstarch dissolved in more cold or room temperature broth (otherwise the

cornstarch will lump if added directly to hot liquids) – then bring back to a boil to activate the full thickening power of the starch. Or instead, at this point you could partially or fully purée the soup to give it more thickness – a handheld immersion blender will do the trick nicely.

6. Choose one or a few ingredients to garnish with. A garnish is anything that compliments in flavour (so it tastes good) but also contrasts in colour (so it stands out). If you are adding a garnish that includes seasoning (like crumbled tortilla chips or crackers, for example) then keep that in mind when you are seasoning to taste in the previous step.

RECIPE NOTES

Spicy Seashore Stew – makes approximately 12 cups
"A big and chunky fish stew"

1 tbsp canola oil
1 small onion, diced small
4 cloves of garlic, minced
2 tsp salt
1/2 tsp pepper
1 – 798ml can diced tomatoes
2 cups tomato juice
1 cup clam juice or clam nectar
2 tsp dried basil
1 tsp (or more) Sambal Oelek
3 cups fresh (from frozen is fine) tortellini
454g fresh fish filets, or thawed from frozen
12 live clams
12 live mussels
1/2 cup chopped fresh parsley
3 tsp sugar
Juice of 1/2 to 1 lemon, zest reserved
Salt, pepper, and sugar to season

1. Heat a large pot over medium heat. Add the oil and then the onion, garlic, salt, and pepper and cook for approximately 2 to 3 minutes until soft.
2. Add tomatoes, tomato juice, clam juice, basil, and Sambal Oelek. Bring to a boil over medium high heat. Add the tortellini and cook for approximately 7 minutes while reducing the heat to medium as it cooks.
3. Cut the fish fillets into large chunks.
4. Add the fish, clams, mussels and cook for approximately 3-4 minutes until the fish is cooked, and the clams and mussels have opened.
5. Gently stir in the parsley, sugar, and lemon juice to taste while trying not to break up the chunks of fish. Re-season with more salt & pepper if desired and serve immediately, garnished with the reserved lemon zest.

Turkey Carcass Soup – makes approximately 10 cups

"Soup is the perfect thing to make with your residual turkey carcass leftover from your turkey dinner. This is based on a carcass from a 7kg turkey."

1 turkey carcass
1 large onion, diced large, trimmings reserved
3 small carrots, sliced into 1/2-inch coins, trimmings reserved
2 large celery stalks, sliced into 1/2-inch pieces, trimmings reserved
6 garlic cloves, chopped, trimmings reserved
10 cups cold water
4 bay leaves
2.5 teaspoons salt
1/2 teaspoon pepper
1.5 cups small pasta shapes

1. Brown the carcass by either grilling direct over charcoal; or over medium/high heat on a gas/propane grill; or in a 450-degree Fahrenheit oven. This step is to create more flavour and colour in your soup.
2. Break the browned, slightly charred carcass into 4 or 5 large pieces and put it in a soup pot. Add the reserved trimmings only of the onion, carrot, celery, and garlic. Cover with the 10 cups cold water and add the bay leaves. Bring to a slight boil over medium-high heat. Cover with the lid slightly ajar and reduce heat to low, to just maintain a slight simmer. Simmer like this for 2.5 hours.
3. Using a large slotted spoon, strain all the big pieces out into a large bowl and set aside.
4. Pour the remaining pot contents through a fine wire strainer into a separate large container – you should have approximately 8 cups of broth.
5. Pour the 8 cups of broth back into the pot. Add the cut pieces of onion, carrot, celery and garlic (these vegetables combined should be about 4 cups worth). Pick through the big pieces (reserved from step 3) to get the chunks of residual turkey meat (about 1.5 to 2 cups) and add to the pot along with the salt and pepper.
6. Bring to a boil over medium-high heat. Cover with the lid slightly ajar and reduce heat to low, to just maintain a slight simmer. Simmer like this for 15 minutes until the carrots become slightly tender.
7. Bring back to a boil over medium-high heat, add the pasta, and cook until desired doneness of the pasta, approximately 8 to 12 minutes, depending on the pasta shape/size. Serve immediately.

PASTA

Fresh Pasta from Scratch – Makes approximately 1 pound

10oz (approx. 2 cups sifted) 00 Flour or all-purpose flour
2 large eggs
4 large egg yolks
1 teaspoon salt
Extra flour for dusting

1. Mound the flour on a countertop and make a well in the center large enough for the rest of the ingredients.
2. Add the eggs, egg yolks, and salt to the well. Scramble the eggs with a fork and slowly start incorporating the flour. Keep mixing with a fork while continuing to incorporate more flour until you cannot mix with a fork any longer. Continue to mix by hand for a couple of minutes until it comes together in one mass. You may need to add a bit of water if it is too dry or a bit more flour if it is too wet. It should be firm and holding together but not sticky.
3. Knead by hand for approximately 10 minutes until smooth. Shape into a ball, cover with plastic wrap and let sit at room temperature for at least 1 hour. Or alternatively up to 3 hours in the refrigerator.
4. Cut dough into 4 equal pieces and work with one piece at a time while keeping the others covered. Set your pasta machine to the widest setting. Hand shape the piece of dough into an approximate rectangle and feed it through the machine. Fold it over and pass it through again. Dust it with a bit of flour now and run it through the 2nd setting twice.
5. Continue to run it through the machine once each on the ramining settings of the rollers until desired thickness is reached.
6. Stop when the pasta has reached the desired thickness, dust liberally with flour and cut into the desired shape(s). Dust one more time with flour and set aside covered with plastic wrap until all the pasta dough is rolled and cut.
7. Bring salted water to a boil and then add the fresh pasta, stirring immediately and cook until done – anywhere from 1 to 5 minutes depending on the thickness you have chosen. Toss with your favorite sauce and enjoy!

Bolognese Pasta Sauce – Makes approximately 12 cups of sauce

"A Bolognese sauce is an Italian pasta sauce that always includes white wine as an ingredient. The meat consistency is very fine resulting in a very smooth sauce. A longer cook for this sauce but well worth the time and effort."

1/4 cup extra virgin olive oil
2 medium onions, diced very small
2 medium carrots, diced very small
2 stalks of celery, diced very small
6 – 8 garlic cloves, minced
2 tablespoons dried basil
1 tablespoon fennel seeds
1 tablespoon salt
1.5 pounds (680g) ground beef
1.5 pounds (680g) ground pork
1.5 cups white wine
2 – 798ml cans diced tomatoes
2 cups chicken broth/stock
6 bay leaves
1/2 teaspoon crushed red pepper flakes
1/2 teaspoon ground cinnamon
1 – 156ml can tomato paste
3 tablespoons white sugar

1. Heat a large Dutch oven, or large pot, over medium heat. Add the oil, onions, carrots, celery, garlic, basil, fennel seeds, and salt. Stir to combine and cook until soft and fragrant, while stirring occasionally, approximately 8 to 10 minutes.
2. While the vegetables are cooking, put the beef and pork in a large bowl with the wine. Thoroughly mix together (with your hands is best) until you get a completely homogenous mixture and there are no large chunks of meat.
3. Add the meat/wine mixture to the pot with the vegetables and cook until meat no longer looks raw, about 5 minutes. Make sure to stir constantly during this process to ensure that the meat does not clump.

4. Increase the heat to medium-high and cook to reduce all the liquid from the pot, while stirring consistently, until the meat is fully cooked and you hear a sizzling sound, approximately 20 to 25 more minutes.
5. Add the tomatoes, broth/stock, bay leaves, red pepper flakes, and cinnamon. Stir to combine and bring to a boil. Turn the heat down to maintain a low simmer for about 2 hours with the lid slightly ajar. Check periodically and stir, to make sure the sauce is not getting too thick.
6. To finish, stir in the tomato paste and the sugar. Season to taste with salt and pepper. Serve immediately with your favourite pasta shape and garnish with freshly grated Parmigiano Reggiano.

Italian Meatballs – Makes approximately 25 to 30 meatballs
"The perfect addition to your pasta sauce to make spaghetti & meatballs"

250g ground chuck (or ground beef)
250g ground pork
1 large egg
1/4 cup fine breadcrumbs
1/4 cup finely grated parmesan cheese
2 tablespoons minced onion
1 tablespoon finely crushed or minced garlic
1 tablespoon dried basil
2 teaspoons red wine vinegar
1 teaspoon salt
1/2 teaspoon pepper

1. Preheat oven to 400 degrees Fahrenheit. Line a baking sheet with parchment paper or spray with baking spray and set aside.
2. In a large bowl, combine all the ingredients together thoroughly. Roll bits of the mixture into small meatballs approximately 3/4 inch in size and place them on the prepared baking sheet. You should have approximately 25 to 30 meatballs.
3. Bake in the preheated oven for approximately 20 minutes, or until their internal temperature reaches 160 degrees Fahrenheit (71 degrees Celsius). Add to your favorite tomato pasta sauce and enjoy!

Potato Gnocchi from Scratch – makes approximately 1.5 pounds

"No matter how you pronounce it, Gnocchi is a potato based Italian pasta that is shaped like little dumplings and tastes amazing. The ridges and indentations of the finished shapes help to hold sauce. If the potatoes are fresh, then the flour needs to be packed. If the potatoes are older (and thus drier) you won't need as much flour."

1-pound (454g) russet potatoes, peeled
1.5 packed cups all-purpose flour
2.25 teaspoons baking powder
1.5 teaspoons salt
1 large egg
Extra flour for dusting/shaping

1. Diced the peeled potatoes into approximately 1/2 inch cubes. Steam for 20 to 25 minutes until tender.
2. For best results place the cooked potatoes through a ricer into a mixing bowl for a fine texture. Alternatively you can thoroughly mash the cooked potatoes, or push the potatoes through a wire strainer, but ricing is better. Let cool slightly before proceeding to the next step.
3. Add the flour, baking powder, salt, and egg to the potatoes. Stir until the dough just starts coming together. Then knead for approximately 2 minutes until a smooth (not sticky) dough is formed. If the dough is sticky, add a bit more flour. If the dough is too dry, wet your hands with a bit of water. Unlike regular homemade pasta, don't knead your gnocchi dough too long otherwise they will become tough.
4. Divide the dough into 8 equal pieces. Working with 1 piece at a time, shape and roll it into a 1/2 inch diameter long rope shape. Cut the shape into 1/2 inch pieces and gently toss in extra flour to keep from sticking to each other. With 2 fingers push each gnocchi piece against a gnocchi paddle (or the tines of a fork works well, or the texture of a cheese grater) to create indents and ridges.
5. Bring salted water to a boil. Boil 1/4 or 1/2 of the gnocchi recipe at a time, boiling for approximately 3 minutes. Use a large slotted spoon to transfer the cooked gnocchi to a strainer. Then add more gnocchi to the boiling water. Add drained gnocchi to desired sauce to coat. Serve immediately.

Mediterranean Linguine

"A rosé pasta dish made with both fresh & sun-dried tomatoes. Flambéed with brandy and finished with fresh basil. Soft Green Peppercorns are soft peppercorns that come in a can or a jar and are sometimes hard to find. Specialty food stores usually have them, but you should call around first. I highly recommend using them in this recipe!"

300g dry linguine
2 tablespoons olive oil
1 large tomato, sliced into thin strips
1/2 cup oil packed sun-dried tomatoes, drained and sliced thin
1/2 cup thinly sliced red onion
2 tablespoons canned soft green peppercorns - *optional
8 cloves garlic, finely minced, or crushed into a paste
2 tablespoons fresh lemon juice
1 tablespoon white sugar
2 teaspoons salt
1/2 teaspoon pepper
1 cup whipping cream
1/4 cup brandy
1/4 cup chopped fresh basil

1. Boil the pasta to desired doneness.
2. In a bowl combine the olive oil, tomato, sun-dried tomato, onion, peppercorns, garlic, lemon juice, sugar, salt, and pepper.
3. Halfway through the cooking process of the pasta, heat a large pan over medium high heat. When hot add the bowl of ingredients from step 2 and cook while stirring occasionally for approximately 2 to 3 minutes.
4. Stir in the cream and bring to a boil. At the moment when it just reaches a boil, carefully add the brandy and carefully ignite with a long lighter or match. Shake the pan lightly until the flames subside and sauce thickens slightly.
5. Drain the pasta in a colander and then toss the pasta in the sauce with the fresh basil. Serve immediately.

Makes 4 portions

Lamb Ragu Tortiglioni

"A Ragu is a meatier pasta sauce with less tomato and always made with red wine. Tortiglioni pasta is like Rigatoni but larger with spiral grooves, but any big pasta shapes will work like: Penne, Rigatoni, Rotini, etc. You will want the carrot and celery to be quite fine, so pulsing in a food processor will make quick work of those 2 ingredients."

2 tablespoons extra virgin olive oil
500g ground lamb (or ground beef if you prefer instead)
1 teaspoon salt
1/2 teaspoon pepper
1 medium onion, diced small
1 medium carrot, finely diced
1 celery stalk, finely diced
6 garlic cloves, minced
1 teaspoon dried thyme
1 teaspoon dried rosemary
2 bay leaves
1 cup red wine
1/2 cup beef broth/stock
2 cups canned tomato sauce
1 tablespoon sugar
375g dry Tortiglioni, or other large pasta shapes (like rigatoni or rotini, for example)
Grated Parmigiano Reggiano, for garnish

1. Place a large pan on medium-high heat and immediately add the olive oil, lamb, salt, and pepper. Cook while breaking the meat apart with a spoon until the meat has browned, approximately 5 minutes.
2. Turn the heat to medium and add the onion, carrot, celery, garlic, thyme, rosemary and bay leaves. Stir to combine and cook while stirring occasionally until the vegetables have softened a bit, approximately 5 minutes.
3. Add the red wine, increase the heat to high and boil until almost all the wine has evaporated, approximately 4 to 5 minutes.

4. Add the beef both/stock, tomato sauce, and sugar. Bring to a boil, then reduce the heat to simmer the sauce uncovered until it has a thick and meaty consistency, approximately 20 minutes.
5. While the sauce is simmering, cook the pasta until desired doneness.
6. Drain the pasta thoroughly and combine immediately with the sauce. Serve immediately, garnished with grated Parmigiano Reggiano cheese.

Makes approximately 4 cups of sauce, or 8 cups total when made with the pasta.

Pastitsio
"A Greek baked pasta dish at its finest"

1 pound lean ground beef
1 large onion, diced small, approximately 2 cups
4 to 6 garlic cloves, minced
1 tablespoon dried oregano
2 to 3 teaspoons salt
1 teaspoon pepper
1 – 156ml can tomato paste
1 – 796ml can of diced tomatoes
1.5 cups full bodied red wine
2 bay leaves
5 tablespoons butter
6 tablespoons flour
3 cups milk
1 teaspoon salt
1/4 teaspoon pepper
1/4 teaspoon ground nutmeg
2 cups crumbled feta cheese
500g macaroni type pasta
3 large eggs

1. Preheat the oven to 350 degrees Fahrenheit and prepare a 9 x 13 x 2.5 inch baking pan with baking spray.
2. Brown the beef in a large pan over medium heat. Stir in the onion, garlic, oregano, 2 teaspoons of the salt, and the 1 teaspoon pepper. Cook until the onion and garlic are soft, approximately 2 to 3 minutes.
3. Stir in the tomato paste, tomatoes, wine, and bay leaves. Bring to a boil and then simmer until sauce consistency is reached, approximately 10 minutes. Season with the other teaspoon of salt if desired and set aside.
4. In a separate pot melt the butter over low heat. Stir in the flour and cook for approximately 5 minutes, stirring occasionally (this removes the starchy taste of the flour). Add the milk gradually, while whisking constantly, until all the milk has been thoroughly incorporated. Stir in the 1 teaspoon salt, 1/4 teaspoon pepper, and nutmeg. Bring to boil

over medium heat, while stirring occasionally, to thicken this white sauce. Remove from the heat, stir in 1 cup of the crumbled feta cheese and set aside.

5. Cook your pasta to desired consistency.

6. In a mixing bowl beat the eggs. Gradually add a small amount (approximately 1/3) of your reserved white sauce into the eggs while whisking constantly – this will temper the eggs to come up in temperature gradually without curdling them. Then mix this tempered egg/sauce mixture back into the remaining white sauce.

7. Assemble your pan as follows: one layer of half of the pasta, top with the remaining cup of crumbled feta cheese, top with the meat sauce, top with the remaining pasta, and finally top with the white sauce.

8. Bake in the oven for approximately 30 minutes to set the eggs in the white sauce. Then broil until lightly browned. Let rest for 10 to 15 minutes before cutting as desired and serve.

Makes 9 large portions or 12 smaller portions

Whiskey Shrimp Pasta

"Flambeeing of the whiskey adds a great flavour dimension to this dish. The stronger the whiskey, the more you'll taste it in the dish – try a smoky scotch for fun!"

2 tbsp butter
1 celery stalk, sliced
1 carrot, sliced
4 – 6 garlic cloves, chopped
1 small onion, chopped
1 pound (454g) raw prawns with shells, peeled, & shells reserved
Salt & pepper
1/2 cup white wine
2 bay leaves
2 teaspoon dried tarragon

----

2 teaspoons canola oil
1 large shallot, sliced thin
1 & 1/4 cups chicken stock, divided
1/4 cup whiskey
3 tablespoons tomato paste
1 cup whipping cream
1 teaspoon salt
1 teaspoon pepper
1 large red bell pepper, cut into thin strips
300g dry pasta of your choice, cooked al dente
Chopped fresh parsley, for garnish

1. Place the butter in a large pan over medium heat and when butter starts to foam, add the celery, carrot, garlic, onion, and the shells from the prawns (reserve the prawn meat for later). Season with salt & pepper and cook for 2 to 3 minutes until the vegetables have softened a bit. Add the wine, bay leaves and tarragon and bring to a boil. Cover & simmer for 10 to 15 minutes to bring out the flavour of the prawn shells. Strain and reserve the liquid in a separate container (discard the solids).

2. Put the pan back on the heat; add the canola oil and sauté the shallot for 1 minute.
3. Add 1/4 cup of the chicken stock to deglaze the pan. Carefully add the whiskey and carefully ignite with a long match/lighter. Flambé until the flames subside.
4. Stir in the tomato paste, and then add the remaining 1 cup of chicken stock, the whipping cream, 1 teaspoon salt, 1 teaspoon pepper, and the reserved liquid from step 1.
5. Heat over medium high heat and reduce until a thick sauce consistency is reached, stirring frequently. Add the prawn meat and the red pepper strips and continue stirring until the prawns are just cooked. Re-season if necessary and toss with the cooked pasta.
6. Garnish with chopped parsley & serve immediately.

Serves 4

Pasta Fresca d'Estate

"Italian for Fresh Summer Pasta. By using a pre-cooked deli chicken, dinner just got a whole lot easier!"

500g of dry pasta shapes (spirali, penne, fussili, etc.)
Salt
1/3 cup butter
6 to 8 garlic cloves, minced
1 medium green zucchini, quartered lengthwise & sliced
4 Roma tomatoes, quartered lengthwise & sliced into chunks
8 yellow cherry tomatoes, quartered
1 whole roasted chicken, deboned & cut into chunks
6 tablespoons extra virgin olive oil
1 tablespoon Kosher Salt, or an infused salt like garlic-rosemary salt
1.5 cups finely grated Parmigiano-Reggiano cheese
Fresh cracked pepper

1. Cook pasta in liberally salted water until 'al dente' firmness (Italian for 'to the tooth', meaning not overcooked; still having some bite/texture to it). Drain in a colander.
2. When the pasta is about half cooked, add the butter to a large deep pan over medium heat, and melt until it just starts to foam. Add the garlic and cook for 2 to 3 minutes until fragrant and cooked, but not browned, stirring constantly to avoid burning.
3. Add the zucchini, Roma tomatoes, cherry tomatoes, and the chicken and toss to coat with the butter and garlic.
4. Add the cooked drained pasta, olive oil, kosher salt, and 1 cup of the parmesan. Toss together thoroughly and serve immediately, garnished with the remaining 1/2 cup of the parmesan and lots of fresh cracked pepper. Buon Appetito!

Makes 6 large portions

RECIPE NOTES

CHINESE TAKE-OUT

Chicken Chop Suey – Makes approximately 4 cups

"Just like Chinese take-out! Chop Suey is a mixture of vegetables along with bite-sized pieces of meat and served with a savoury sauce."

1 tablespoon cornstarch
2 tablespoons soy sauce
2 tablespoons oyster sauce
1 teaspoon sesame oil
3/4 cup chicken broth
2 tablespoons canola oil, divided
1 boneless skinless chicken breast, sliced thin
1/2 medium onion, sliced thin
1 medium carrot, sliced thin on an angle
1 large celery stalk, sliced thin on an angle
3 garlic cloves, chopped
1 tablespoon chopped fresh ginger
1 cup thick sliced fresh cremini mushrooms
2 cups sliced baby bok choy
1 cup fresh bean sprouts

1. In a 2-cup measuring cup, or a small mixing bowl, dissolve the cornstarch in the soy sauce. Then stir in the oyster sauce, sesame oil, and chicken broth. Set aside.
2. Heat up a wok on medium-high to high heat. Add 1 tablespoon of the oil and immediately add the chicken and sauté for 2 minutes, until just starting to brown.
3. Add the other 1 tablespoon of the oil and the onion, carrot, and celery. Followed by the garlic and ginger. Sauté for 1 to 2 minutes until the onions are soft.
4. Add the mushrooms and sauté for 1 to 2 minutes.
5. Add the bok choy and sauté for 1 minute.

Stir in the bean sprouts and then push the whole mixture up the sides up the wok. Stir up the reserved sauce mixture (from step 1), as the cornstarch will have settled on the bottom. Immediately add this sauce mixture to the middle of the wok and bring to a full boil to thicken. Stir everything together and serve immediately.

Almond Chicken

"A classic Chinese Take-Out favourite! An oil thermometer is a must for this recipe. If you can't find almond flour, then substitute with all-purpose flour."

Canola oil for frying
2 boneless skinless chicken breasts, approximately 1-pound (454g) total
6 tablespoons almond flour, divided
1/2 teaspoon salt
1/4 teaspoon pepper
2 tablespoons all-purpose flour
4 tablespoons cornstarch
1/2 teaspoon baking powder
2 large eggs, beaten
Fine Kosher salt or sea salt
1/4 cup chopped blanched almonds, toasted
Shredded iceberg lettuce

1. In a large deep pot, add enough canola oil for about a 2 to 3 inch depth of oil. Heat the oil until you can maintain a consistent temperature of 370 to 380 degrees Fahrenheit.
2. Butterfly cut the thicker part of the chicken breasts to make them more uniform in thickness. Place each chicken breast between two pieces of wax paper or plastic wrap. Using the flat side of a meat tenderizer mallet, flatten the chicken breasts to a uniform thickness of approximately 1/2 inch.
3. On a dinner plate, combine 4 tablespoons of the almond flour with the 1/2 teaspoon salt and 1/4 teaspoon of pepper and set aside.
4. In a large mixing bowl, combine the remaining 2 tablespoons of almond flour with the all-purpose flour, cornstarch, and baking powder. Then whisk in the beaten eggs to make a batter – it should be the consistency of pancake batter.
5. Work with 1 chicken breast at a time as follows: dredge the flattened chicken breast in the seasoned almond flour mixture until lightly coated. Then coat with a thin layer of batter and carefully and slowly add to the hot oil. Fry until golden brown and crispy, approximately 5 minutes total, and turn the chicken over in the oil at the halfway mark.

The internal temperature should be at least 160 degrees Fahrenheit. Once done, transfer to a wire rack and immediately dust with the Kosher salt and sprinkle with some toasted almonds.

6. Once both chicken breasts are done, prepare a serving dish with a layer of shredded iceberg lettuce.

7. Slice the chicken into 1/2-inch strips and place on the lettuce. Sprinkle with any remaining almonds and serve immediately.

Makes approximately 4 servings

Chicken Chow Mein – Makes approximately 6 portions

"The chow mein noodles are often called "Steamed Chow Mein Noodles" and they are usually found in the deli section (refrigerated) of your major grocery store."

454g (1 pound) boneless, skinless chicken thighs
Salt & pepper
454g (1 pound) fresh chow mein noodles
3 tablespoons grape seed oil, or peanut oil
3 cups shredded green cabbage
2 small carrots, cut into matchstick shapes
3 cloves garlic, chopped
1 small onion, sliced thin
4 teaspoons cornstarch
1/2 cup chicken broth
3 tablespoons soy sauce
3 tablespoons oyster sauce
4 teaspoons white sugar
1 tablespoon sesame oil
1 bunch green onions, sliced into 1-inch lengths
Soy sauce to season, if desired

1. Slice the chicken thighs into thin strips. Dust lightly with salt & pepper and set aside.
2. Boil the chow mein noodles for 3 minutes (or check package directions). Let drain in colander while preparing the remaining steps.
3. Heat a wok over medium-high to high heat. Add 1 tbsp oil and then approximately one third of the chicken. Cook through until slightly browned. Remove from wok and repeat two more times with remaining oil and chicken.
4. Put all the cooked chicken back into the hot wok. Add the cabbage, carrots, garlic, and onion. Sauté for 2 or 3 minutes.
5. Stir in the drained noodles.
6. Dissolve the cornstarch in the chicken broth and combine with the 3 tablespoons soy sauce, oyster sauce, sugar, and sesame oil. Stir this sauce mixture into your chow mein along with the green onions. Keep tossing until thoroughly coated and warmed through.

Chicken Shanghai Chow Mein

"If you don't have a wok, a large pan will work just fine"

454g (1 pound) boneless, skinless chicken thighs
454g (1 pound) fresh shanghai noodles
3 tablespoons grape seed oil, or canola oil
3 cloves garlic, chopped
1 tablespoon fresh ginger, minced or grated
1.5 cups shredded cabbage (savoy or sui choy)
1.5 cups bean sprouts
3 to 4 shitake mushrooms, stems discarded, sliced
1 bunch green onions, sliced into 1-inch lengths
1 small carrot, grated
5 tablespoons hoisin sauce
5 tablespoons black bean sauce
1/2 cup chicken broth
1 to 2 tablespoons sesame oil
Soy sauce to season, if desired

1. Slice the chicken thighs into thin strips and set aside.
2. Boil the shanghai noodles until they have separated from each other, then drain and rinse with cold water until cooled. Let drain while preparing recipe.
3. Heat a wok over medium-high to high heat. Add 1 tbsp oil and then approximately one third of the chicken. Cook through until slightly browned. Remove from wok and repeat two more times with remaining oil and chicken.
4. Put all the cooked chicken back into the hot wok. Add the garlic, ginger, cabbage, bean sprouts, mushrooms, green onions, and carrot. Sauté for two or three minutes.
5. Stir in the drained noodles. Add the hoisin sauce, black bean sauce, chicken broth, and sesame oil. Stir until thoroughly coated and warmed through.
6. Season with soy sauce to taste, if desired.

Makes 4 to 6 portions

Chicken Fried Rice

"Another classic Chinese Take-Out favourite. If you have it, a higher heat oil, like extra virgin avocado oil, is even better than canola oil."

4 teaspoons canola oil, separated
2 large eggs, beaten
3/4-pound (340g) chicken breast or thigh, boneless skinless, cut into small pieces
Salt & pepper
1/2 cup small diced onion
1 small carrot, diced small, approximately 1/3 cup
1 tablespoon finely minced or grated ginger
1 cup frozen peas
4 cups cold pre-cooked rice
3 garlic cloves, finely minced or crushed in garlic press
1 teaspoon chicken stock paste*
1 tablespoon oyster sauce
2 tablespoons soy sauce
1/2 teaspoon ground turmeric
1 tablespoon butter
1 tablespoon sesame oil
4 green onions, sliced 1/4 inch

1. Heat a large pan or wok over medium-high heat. Add 2 teaspoons of the canola oil and then the beaten eggs. Cook for about 30 seconds while breaking up until completely cooked into small bits.
2. Add the chicken to the egg and season lightly with some salt & pepper. Cook while stirring frequently for about 2 minutes until chicken is mostly cooked.
3. Add the other 2 teaspoons canola oil, then the onion, carrot, and ginger. Cook, stirring frequently, until onion and carrot are mostly soft, approximately 2 minutes.
4. Stir in the frozen peas. Thoroughly stir in the rice and garlic and cook for about 1 minute, making sure to break up any lumps of rice.
5. In a small bowl, whisk the chicken stock paste together with the oyster sauce. Then whisk in the soy sauce to this mixture. Stir this mixture

thoroughly into the rice with the turmeric and cook for about 1 more minute until the rice is completely heated, stirring frequently.

6. Stir in the butter, sesame oil, and green onions. Continue stirring until the butter has completely melted. Season to taste with more soy sauce (or salt & pepper) if desired and serve immediately.

Makes approximately 6 cups

---

*Chicken stock paste is chicken broth that has been reduced down to a concentrated paste form. The most common brand found at your local grocery stores is "Better Than Bouillon" Chicken Base – in small glass jars. Once opened this will last 1 year easily in your refrigerator.

Egg Rolls

"You can use either Egg Roll Wrappers or Spring Roll Wrappers for this recipe. I prefer the Spring Roll Wrappers as they are thinner, come out crispier, and are more like the egg rolls you get with Chinese Take-Out. A standard sized cheese grater will make quick work out of most of your prep for this recipe. An oil thermometer is a must for this recipe."

100g (3.5oz) vermicelli rice noodles
454g (1 pound) lean ground pork
2 teaspoons canola or vegetable oil
3 teaspoons salt, separated
1 teaspoon pepper
2 teaspoons Chinese 5-spice powder, separated
2 packed cups grated cabbage
1 medium/large carrot, grated, approximately 1 packed cup
1 small onion, grated, approximately 1/2 packed cup
6 garlic cloves, finely minced or crushed to a paste
3 tablespoons grated fresh ginger
2 tablespoons soy sauce
2 tablespoons oyster sauce
1 tablespoon sesame oil
2 eggs, beaten
Canola oil for frying
454g (1 pound) package of fresh spring roll wrappers (8x8 inches in size)
-or-
2 – 454g packages of fresh egg roll wrappers (5x5 inches in size)

1. Put vermicelli noodles in a stainless-steel bowl and pour boiling water over them. Separate with a fork and let stand for 5 minutes. Then drain in wire mesh strainer and rinse with cold water. Let stand draining while you continue with the recipe.
2. In a large pan over medium-high heat, add the pork, 2 teaspoons canola oil, 2 teaspoons of the salt, pepper, and 1 teaspoon of the 5-spice powder. Cook, stirring frequently, until browned and a little crispy, about 7-10 minutes. Remove with a slotted spoon and set aside in a large bowl.

3. Turn the heat to medium and add the cabbage, carrot, onion, garlic, ginger, soy sauce, the last 1 teaspoon of the salt, and the other 1 teaspoon of the 5-spice powder. Cook, stirring occasionally, until tender, about 6-8 minutes. Transfer this cabbage mixture to the large bowl with the pork. Stir in the oyster sauce and sesame oil.

4. Place the drained vermicelli noodles on a cutting board and cut into small pieces (about 1 inch) and mix into pork/cabbage mixture to complete the filling. This will be approximately 6 cups of filling.

5. Separate your wrappers. If using the larger spring roll wrappers you will use 1/3 cup filling per wrapper. If using the smaller egg roll wrappers you will use 3-4 tablespoons of filling per wrapper. Place the wrapper with 1 point facing you (looks like a diamond). Place 1 portion of the filling just below the center of the wrapper. Brush the top 2 edges with some beaten egg. Wrap the bottom point of the wrapper over the filling, tuck the side points of the wrapper over the filling, and then roll away from you to seal the egg roll (make sure that the filling is fairly tightly encased with the wrap as you roll to make a good seal). Continue until all filling is used (you will have some leftover wrappers). Set these wrapped egg rolls on a tray.

6. In a large deep pot, add enough canola oil for about a 2 to 3 inch depth of oil. Heat the oil until you can maintain a consistent temperature of 350 to 375 degrees Fahrenheit.

7. Working in batches, carefully place 3 to 4 rolls in the hot oil, one at a time. Fry until golden brown and crispy: 3 minutes for spring roll wrappers, and approximately 4 to 5 minutes for egg roll wrappers. Set aside on a wire rack when done.

8. Repeat previous step until all the rolls are cooked. Serve with your favorite plum sauce and enjoy!

Makes 18 rolls if you use spring roll wrappers, or 24 rolls with egg roll wrappers

Ginger Beef

"A classic Chinese Take-Out favourite! An oil thermometer is a must for this recipe."

1 tablespoon canola oil
1 medium onion, sliced thin
3/4 teaspoon salt
3 tablespoons cornstarch
5 tablespoons soy sauce
1 cup beef broth
1/2 cup dark brown sugar
7 tablespoons liquid honey
3 tablespoons minced fresh ginger
3 tablespoons white vinegar
1/4 to 3/4 teaspoon red chili flakes
1 small red bell pepper, cut into small strips
Canola oil for frying
1/2 cup cornstarch
3 tablespoons all-purpose flour
2 teaspoons baking powder
2 teaspoons salt
2 teaspoons white sugar
1/2 teaspoon garlic powder
1/2 teaspoon ground ginger (powder)
7 tablespoons cold water
800g flank steak, cut into thin, short strips
3 green onions, sliced on an angle, for garnish
Sesame seeds, for garnish

8. Heat a large pan or wok over medium heat. Add the 1 tablespoon of canola oil and then the onion slices and 3/4 teaspoon of salt. Cook for 3-4 minutes until the onion is tender, stirring occasionally.
9. Dissolve the 3 tablespoons of cornstarch in the soy sauce in a mixing bowl. Then to this cornstarch mixture stir in the beef broth, brown sugar, honey, fresh ginger, vinegar, and chili flakes. Pour this mixture in the pan with the cooked onions. Increase heat to bring to a full boil to thicken the sauce. Turn off the heat and stir in the red bell pepper.

10. Meanwhile, in a large deep pot, add enough canola oil for about a 2 to 3 inch depth of oil. Heat the oil until you can maintain a consistent temperature of 350 to 375 degrees Fahrenheit.

11. In a large mixing bowl, combine the 1/2 cup cornstarch, flour, baking powder, 2 teaspoons salt, 2 teaspoons white sugar, garlic powder, and ground ginger. Then whisk in the cold water to make a batter. Add the beef strips and mix completely by hand so that all the beef strips are coated.

12. Working in batches, quickly and carefully add about a handful of beef strips to the hot oil – it is important to add the beef strips individually so that they stay separate from each other. Fry until golden brown and crispy, approximately 3 minutes. Move the beef strips around a bit in the hot oil as they cook. Once done, transfer to a paper towel lined tray.

13. Repeat step 5 until all the beef is cooked.

14. Combine the sauce and beef together. Garnish with the green onion and sesame seeds. Serve and enjoy!

Makes approximately 6 cups

Honey Garlic Pork

"A classic Chinese Take-Out favourite! An oil thermometer or a deep fryer with a thermostat is a must for this recipe."

3 large garlic cloves, crushed to a paste
2/3 cup liquid honey
1/2 cup chicken broth
1/4 cup apple cider vinegar
2 tablespoons soy sauce
1 tablespoon brown sugar
Canola oil for frying
6 tablespoons all-purpose flour
6 tablespoons cornstarch
1.5 teaspoons baking powder
1.5 teaspoons salt
1.5 teaspoons white sugar
1/2 teaspoon garlic powder
1/2 cup cold water
750g pork tenderloin, cut into bite sized pieces
2 to 3 green onions, sliced 45-degree angle, for garnish

1. To a medium sized pan, add the garlic, honey, chicken broth, vinegar, soy sauce, and brown sugar. Stir to combine. Turn the heat to medium/high to bring to a boil and boil uncovered for approximately 5 to 7 minutes until the sauce has been reduced in volume to make 1 cup of sauce total. Remove from the pan and let stand off the heat.
2. In a large deep pot, add enough canola oil for about a 2 to 3 inch depth of oil. Heat the oil until you can maintain a consistent temperature of 350 to 375 degrees Fahrenheit.
3. In a large mixing bowl, combine the flour, cornstarch, baking powder, salt, white sugar, and garlic powder. Then whisk in the cold water to make a batter. Add the pork pieces and mix completely by hand so that all the pork pieces are coated.
4. Working in batches, quickly and carefully add about 10 to 15 battered pork pieces to the hot oil – it is important to add the pork pieces individually so that they stay separate from each other. Fry until golden

brown and crispy, approximately 4 minutes. Move the pork pieces around a bit in the hot oil as they cook. Once done, transfer to a paper towel lined tray.

5. Repeat step 4 until all the pork is cooked.
6. Heat a large pan over medium/high heat and add all the cooked pork to the pan. Drizzle the reserved sauce from step 1 over the pork and cook for approximately 2 minutes while stirring and tossing the pork in the sauce, until the sauce becomes a bit more syrupy and coats the pork thoroughly.
7. Transfer to a serving dish, garnish with the green onions, and enjoy!

Makes approximately 6 cups

Sweet & Sour Chicken Balls

"A classic Chinese Take-Out favourite! An oil thermometer or a deep fryer with a thermostat is a must for this recipe."

398ml can of pineapple tidbits or chunks, drained and juice reserved
3 tablespoons cornstarch
1.25 cups white sugar
3/4 cup white vinegar
1/2 cup ketchup
1/3 cup dark brown sugar
1 teaspoon salt
1 tablespoon canola oil
1 small red onion, cut into large pieces
Canola oil for frying
1/2 cup all-purpose flour
1/2 cup cornstarch
2 teaspoons baking powder
2 teaspoons salt
2 teaspoons white sugar
1/2 teaspoon garlic powder
1/2 cup & 2 tablespoons cold water
1kg chicken breast filets, or chicken breasts, cut into bite sized pieces

1. Mix the reserved pineapple juice (should be approximately 2/3 cup of juice) with the 3 tablespoons of cornstarch in a medium mixing bowl. Then mix in the 1.25 cups white sugar, white vinegar, ketchup, brown sugar, and the 1 teaspoon of salt and set aside. Reserve the pineapple pieces separately.
2. Heat a large pan or wok over medium-high heat. Add the 1 tablespoon of canola oil and then the onion pieces. Sauté for 1 minute.
3. Add the reserved sauce mixture from step 1 to the pan and bring to a full rolling boil to completely thicken the sauce, stirring consistently. Once thickened, remove from the heat, stir in the reserved pineapple, and set aside.

4. In a large deep pot, add enough canola oil for about a 2 to 3 inch depth of oil. Heat the oil until you can maintain a consistent temperature of 350 to 375 degrees Fahrenheit.
5. In a large mixing bowl, combine the flour, 1/2 cup cornstarch, baking powder, 2 teaspoons salt, 2 teaspoons white sugar, and garlic powder. Then whisk in the cold water to make a batter. Add the chicken pieces and mix completely by hand so that all the chicken pieces are coated.
6. Working in batches, quickly and carefully add about 10 to 15 chicken pieces to the hot oil – it is important to add the chicken pieces individually so that they stay separate from each other. Fry until golden brown and crispy, approximately 4 minutes. Move the chicken pieces around a bit in the hot oil as they cook. Once done, transfer to a paper towel lined tray.
7. Repeat step 6 until all the chicken is cooked.
8. Combine the sauce and chicken together in a serving dish and enjoy!

Makes approximately 10 cups

Wontons

"Wontons that taste just like take-out. Use them in Wonton Soup or deep fry them and serve with Sweet & Sour Sauce. The best flavour is with equal amounts of pork and prawns as stated, but use all pork, or all prawns instead if preferred. A typical 400g pack of wonton wrappers will have anywhere from 55-60 wrappers."

340g ground medium pork
340g raw shelled & deveined prawns, finely chopped
2 green onions, sliced thin
1 tablespoon soy sauce
1 tablespoon finely minced or grated ginger
2 cloves of garlic, finely minced
2 teaspoons cornstarch
1 teaspoon sesame oil
1 teaspoon sugar
1 teaspoon salt
1/4 teaspoon ground white pepper
75 fresh wonton wrappers

1. In a mixing bowl, add the pork, prawns, green onions, soy sauce, ginger, garlic, cornstarch, sesame oil, sugar, salt, and white pepper. Mix thoroughly with your hand until well combined.
2. Working with one wonton wrapper at a time, place a wrapper on the counter in front of you aligned with one point of the square pointing towards you. Place a slightly rounded teaspoon of filling in the center of the wonton wrapper. Have a small dish of water standing by. With your finger, slightly wet the 2 edges on the wonton wrapper that are farthest away from you. Fold up the bottom point of the wrapper, over the filling, to match up with the top point and press to seal. Then working with your fingers, seal the left & right edges together starting from the sealed top point and working downwards, while also making sure that you're not trapping air in the sealed wonton. Gather and press the sealed edges together at the top to create little "pouches".
3. Place each filled sealed wonton on a parchment lined baking tray as they are completed, keeping them separate from each other. Cook from fresh or place the filled baking sheet in the freezer for 2 hours. If

freezing, transfer the individually frozen wontons to a sealed container and then place back in the freezer for future use and use within 3 months.

Makes 75 wontons

Wonton Soup

"Please see my recipe for fresh homemade wontons or use pre-made store bought wontons"

4 green onions
6 cups chicken broth
3 to 4 thin slices of ginger
1 teaspoon sesame oil
1 tablespoon soy sauce
36 prepared wontons

1. Cut the green onions to separate the green parts from the white parts. Thinly slice the green parts at a 45-degree angle and set aside to reserve for garnish. Place the white parts, whole, in a pot or large saucepan.
2. To that pot or large saucepan, add the chicken broth, ginger, and sesame oil. Bring to a boil, then turn down to a simmer. Cover and let simmer for 15 minutes to infuse the chicken broth with the onion and ginger flavours.
3. Remove the cover and strain out the onion and ginger pieces. Stir in the soy sauce and increase the heat to bring back to a boil. Add the prepared wontons and cook for 2 to 3 minutes until wontons are fully cooked. Serve immediately, garnished with the reserved angle-cut green onions. Season with more soy sauce, if desired.

Makes 8 cups of soup

BEEF & LAMB

Moist Classic Meatloaf

"The moistest meatloaf you will ever have. A family classic reinvented!"

3 pounds (1.36kg) lean ground beef
3 large eggs
2 onions, finely chopped
2 cloves of garlic, minced
2 cups breadcrumbs
1.5 cups milk
6 tablespoons ketchup
2 tablespoons Worcestershire sauce
3 teaspoons salt
2 teaspoons pepper

Sauce
1 cup ketchup
1/2 cup white sugar
1/4 cup red wine vinegar

1. Preheat oven to 350 degrees Fahrenheit.
2. Prepare 2 standard loaf pans with baking spray, butter, or line with parchment paper.
3. In a large bowl, mix together the meat loaf ingredients: ground beef, eggs, onions, garlic, bread crumbs, milk, 6 tbsp ketchup, Worcestershire, salt, and pepper.
4. Divide this mixture equally between the 2 prepared pans and press down to make an even flat surface on the meat loaves.
5. Mix the 3 sauce ingredients together and distribute evenly over the 2 meat loaves.
6. Bake in the preheated oven until the internal temperature reaches 71 degrees Celsius, or 165 degrees Fahrenheit, approximately 1 hour.
7. Let cool in pans for at least 20 minutes before slicing and serving.

Makes 2 meat loaves

Apple Braised Beef Shanks

"Topping with a mild crumbled blue cheese extremely compliments this dish. Apples, blue cheese, and the beef flavours marry together immensely."

4 large bone-in beef shank steaks, approximately 1.5kg total
Salt & pepper
1 to 2 tablespoons canola oil
1 small onion, chopped
1 small carrot, chopped
1 celery stalk, chopped
3 to 4 large garlic cloves, chopped
1 cup red wine
1 cup beef broth
2 stalks fresh rosemary
2 to 3 bay leaves
4 Granny Smith apples
3 tablespoons & 1 teaspoon brown sugar
1/2 tsp beef stock paste*
50g mild blue cheese, crumbled

1. Preheat oven to 325 degrees F. Prepare apples by peeling and coring them, and then cut them eighths (cut in half, then cut each half in half to make 4 quarters, and then cut each quarter in half to make 8 pieces per apple) and set aside.
2. Heat a large pan over medium-high to high heat, and have a roasting pan (equipped with a lid) standing by.
3. Salt and pepper the beef shanks steaks on both sides. Add the oil to the hot pan and sear the steaks on both sides until brown. Do not crowd the pan as this will inhibit the searing process. Set the seared steaks in the roasting pan in a single layer.
4. Turn the pan heat off and add the onion, carrot, celery, garlic and 1/2 cup of the red wine. Stir to coat and cook slightly, approximately 2 minutes. Transfer this mixture to the roasting pan with the steaks, arranging this mixture in-between the steaks (not on top of the steaks). Pour the remaining 1/2 cup of wine and the 1 cup beef broth over the steaks and nestle the rosemary stalks and the bay leaves in this liquid.

5. Toss the cut apple pieces with the 3 tbsp brown sugar until coated and arrange them on the steaks (not in the liquid). Cover the roasting pan and cook in the oven until meat is very tender, approximately 2 hours.

6. Gently remove the steaks while keeping the cooked apples on them, and plate them. Working quickly, strain the sauce through a wire mesh strainer (to remove the cooked vegetables and herbs, and discard them) and then boil this liquid down to half the volume, while stirring in the remaining 1 tsp brown sugar and the 1/2 tsp beef stock paste. This will be an intensely flavoured sauce.

7. Pour the reduced sauce over the plated steaks/apples, and top with the crumbled blue cheese. Serving Suggestion: Serve Butternut Mash (see Side Dish Chapter)

Makes 4 large portions

* Beef stock paste is beef broth that has been reduced down to a concentrated paste form. The most common brand found at your local grocery stores is "Better Than Bouillon" Chicken Base – in small glass jars. Once opened this will last 1 year easily in your refrigerator.

Beef & Black Bean Enchiladas

1.5 pounds (680g) lean ground beef
1 cup small diced onion
6 to 8 garlic cloves, minced
2 tablespoons Mexican chili powder
1 tablespoon dried oregano
1 tablespoon dried ground cumin
2 teaspoons salt
1/2 teaspoon pepper
3 tablespoons canned green chilies
2 tablespoons dark brown sugar
2 cups canned crushed tomatoes (divided into 2 parts)
1 – 398ml can black beans, rinsed & drained
6 large soft flour tortillas
340g old cheddar, grated
Toppings:
Sour cream
Sliced canned black olives, drained
Small diced fresh tomatoes
Green onions, sliced

1. Preheat oven to 350 degrees Fahrenheit and prepare a 9x13 pan with baking spray.
2. Brown the beef in a large frying pan over medium to medium-high heat.
3. Add the diced onion, garlic, chili powder, oregano, cumin, salt, pepper, green chilies, brown sugar and only 1 cup of the crushed tomatoes. Stir to combine and cook for approximately 2 to 3 minutes, over medium heat, until the onions are softened.
4. Remove 1 cup of this cooked meat sauce and in a small bowl mix it with the second cup of crushed tomatoes – set aside. We will call this the "meat/tomato mixture".
5. Stir in the black beans to the remaining meat sauce in the pan and remove from the heat. We will call the "meat/bean mixture".

6. Set out the 6 tortillas on the counter and equally spoon out all of the "meat/bean mixture" onto them.
7. Spread 1 cup of the reserved "meat/tomato mixture" into the prepared empty 9x13 pan.
8. Roll up each tortilla and place them in the pan (seam side down) one at a time, until all 6 are in the pan.
9. Spread the remaining "meat/tomato mixture" down the center on the enchiladas and top evenly with the grated cheese.
10. Bake for 30 minutes until hot and the cheese has melted/browned.
11. Top with sour cream, black olives, tomatoes, and green onions, either while still in the pan or individually.

Makes 6 Portions

Lamb Shanks in BBQ Sauce

"Lamb shanks two ways: In the oven or a pressure cooker. Either way these lamb shanks are incredibly tender and flavourful."

3 small lamb shanks (1kg total)
2-3 tablespoons canola oil
Salt & pepper
3 sprigs fresh rosemary, chopped
6 garlic cloves, chopped
3 small shallots, chopped – or – 1/2 cup chopped onion
2 tablespoons minced fresh ginger
1 cup red wine
3 to 6 tablespoons of your favourite Barbeque Sauce
1/2 teaspoon salt
1/2 teaspoon pepper
1 to 1.5 teaspoons white sugar
1 tablespoons cornstarch dissolved in 2 tablespoons red wine

OVEN METHOD

1. Preheat oven to 300 degrees Fahrenheit.
2. Heat an oven proof pan over medium-high heat. Coat the lamb shanks with 1 tbsp of the oil and season with salt and pepper. When the pan is hot, add 1 tbsp of oil to the pan and then sear the lamb shanks on all sides and ends.
3. Once the lamb is seared, remove the lamb from the pan and remove pan from the heat to cool down a bit. Score the shanks deeply in a number of spots and stuff with rosemary.
4. Add one more tbsp of oil to the pan (if needed) along with the garlic, shallots, and ginger. Cook for 1 minute. If the pan is too cool, place it on medium heat.
5. Add the wine to the pan and stir to deglaze.
6. Add the lamb shanks back to the pan and spread 1 to 2 tbsp of barbeque sauce on the top of each shank.
7. Cover the pan and bake in the oven for approximately 90 minutes until the meat is tender and mostly releasing from the bones.

8. Remove the lamb shanks from the pan and set aside to rest.
9. While lamb is resting, finish the sauce by adding 1/2 teaspoon salt, 1/2 teaspoon pepper, sugar, and dissolved cornstarch. Bring to a boil on the stovetop to thicken and then serve over the lamb shanks.

PRESSURE COOKER METHOD
1. Preheat pressure cooker pot over medium-high heat. Coat the lamb shanks with 1 tbsp of the oil and season with salt and pepper. When the pot is hot, add 1 tbsp of oil to the pot and then sear the lamb shanks on all sides and ends.
2. Once the lamb is seared, remove the lamb from the pot and remove pot from the heat to cool down a bit. Score the shanks deeply in a number of spots and stuff with rosemary.
3. Add one more tbsp of oil to the pot (if needed) along with the garlic, shallots, and ginger. Cook for 1 minute. If the pot is too cool, place it on medium heat.
4. Add the wine to the pot and stir to deglaze.
5. Add the lamb shanks back to the pot and spread 1 to 2 tbsp of barbeque sauce on the top of each shank.
6. Close the pressure cooker, turn the heat to high, and cook under pressure for 30 minutes, reducing heat and timing from when pressure is reached. Remove from the heat source, and allow pressure to drop naturally. Open the pressure cooker once pressure has dropped completely. Remove the lamb shanks from the pressure cooker and set aside to rest.
7. While lamb is resting, finish the sauce by adding 1/2 teaspoon salt, 1/2 teaspoon pepper, sugar and dissolved cornstarch. Bring to a boil to thicken and then serve over the lamb shanks.

Serves approximately 3 – 4

Merlot-Sauced Steak Sandwiches - Makes 2 open-faced sandwiches

"A unique flavourful twist on the classic steak sandwich - served open-faced on naan bread"

1 cup & 2 tablespoons merlot or other full-bodied red wine
1 medium/large shallot, minced
1 garlic clove, minced
1 bay leaf
1/2 teaspoon dried thyme leaves
1/2 teaspoon white sugar
1 – 2 teaspoons cornstarch
Salt & pepper
Vegetable oil
2 thin "fast fry" boneless prime rib steaks
2 slices naan bread
1 - 2 tablespoons butter mixed with 1 crushed garlic clove

1. In a heavy-bottomed small saucepan, put the 1 cup merlot, shallot, garlic, bay leaf, and thyme. Bring to a boil over med-high heat.
2. Lower the heat to medium and reduce until only just over 1/4 cup of liquid remains in the saucepan.
3. Strain the solids from the liquid through a wire mesh strainer and put the liquid back into the saucepan (discard the solids). Add the sugar to this liquid and stir to dissolve.
4. In a small separate bowl, mix the cornstarch with the other 2 tablespoons of merlot.
5. Stir in a very small amount of the cornstarch mixture into the sauce and bring the sauce to a boil over medium heat, stirring constantly. Continue to add just enough of the cornstarch mixture until the sauce looks like a glaze – not too thick!
6. Season to taste with salt & pepper and set the sauce aside.
7. Rub both sides of the steaks with a small amount of oil and season with salt and pepper.
8. Brush the naans with the garlic butter.
9. Sear the steaks in a hot pan or hot grill for approximately 1 to 1.5 minutes per side.

10. Warm the naans in the oven while the steaks are cooking.
11. For each portion serve one naan, top it with a steak and drizzle with 1/2 of the merlot sauce.

Saucy Little Meat Loaves – Makes 6 portions

"My Aunt Shirley used to make something like this for me when I was a kid – one of my favourite meals of hers! Individual meat loaves with a zesty sauce – loaded with flavour."

1.5 pounds (680g) lean ground beef
1 egg
1/2 cup quick oats
1/4 cup minced onion
4 cloves garlic, minced or crushed to a paste
1 tablespoon dark brown sugar
1.5 teaspoons salt
1 teaspoon chili powder
1 teaspoon dried basil leaves
1/2 teaspoon pepper
1 – 680ml can of tomato sauce
1/2 cup blueberry jam or grape jelly
1/4 cup dark brown sugar
4 teaspoons cornstarch
2 teaspoons Worcestershire sauce
1 teaspoon salt
1/4 teaspoon pepper

1. Preheat oven to 400 degrees.
2. Combine the ground beef with the egg, oats, onion, garlic, 1 tablespoon brown sugar, 1.5 teaspoons salt, chili powder, basil, 1/2 teaspoon pepper, and 1/2 cup of the tomato sauce. Shape into 6 ovals (loaves) in a shallow baking dish and bake for 20 minutes.
3. Combine the remaining tomato sauce, jam/jelly, 1/4 cup brown sugar, cornstarch, Worcestershire, 1 teaspoon salt and 1/4 teaspoon pepper in a bowl.
4. At the end of the 20 minute baking time, remove the fat from the pan and pour the sauce mixture over the loaves. Bake 10 minutes longer.

Mexican Casserole

1.5 pounds (680g) lean ground beef
1 cup small diced onion
6 to 8 garlic cloves, minced
2 tablespoons Mexican chili powder
1 tablespoon dried oregano
1 tablespoon dried ground cumin
2 teaspoons salt
1/2 teaspoon pepper
3 tablespoons canned green chilies
2 tablespoons dark brown sugar
1 cup canned crushed tomatoes
1 – 398ml can refried beans
2 cups cooked rice
1 – 398ml can black beans, rinsed & drained
340g old cheddar, grated
Toppings:
Sour cream
Sliced canned black olives, drained
Small diced fresh tomatoes
Green onions, sliced

1. Preheat oven to 350 degrees Fahrenheit and prepare a 9x13 pan with baking spray.
2. Brown the beef in a large frying pan over medium to medium-high heat.
3. Add the diced onion, garlic, chili powder, oregano, cumin, salt, pepper, green chilies, brown sugar and the crushed tomatoes. Stir to combine and cook for approximately 2 to 3 minutes, over medium heat, until the onions are softened. Remove from the heat and set aside.
4. In the prepared 9x13 pan, spread the refried beans evenly to form the base layer of the casserole. On top of this refried bean layer, continue evenly building the casserole with these layers in the following order: cooked rice, reserved meat sauce, black beans, and finally the grated cheddar.

5. Bake for 20 minutes and then top with some crumbled tortilla chips. Continue to bake for 10 more minutes until hot and the cheese has melted/browned.
6. Top with sour cream, black olives, tomatoes, and green onions, either while still in the pan or individually.

Makes 8 to 12 portions

RECIPE NOTES

PORK

Chili-Rubbed Pork with Chow Chow Sauce

"I like this pork recipe done over natural lump charcoal for the best flavour, but a gas/propane grill or an oven will work in a pinch. Makes 6 – 8 portions."

3 tablespoons Mexican chili powder
1.5 tablespoons brown sugar (not golden sugar)
2 teaspoons granulated garlic or garlic powder
2 teaspoons sweet smoked paprika
2 teaspoons salt
2 teaspoons ground cumin
1 teaspoon pepper
1 teaspoon dried oregano
1/2 teaspoon ground cinnamon
1 tablespoon canola oil
2 pork tenderloins, approximately 1kg (2.2 pounds) total
1 recipe of Chow Chow Sauce (see "Sauce Chapter" of this book)

1. Combine the chili powder, brown sugar, garlic, paprika, salt, cumin, pepper, oregano, and cinnamon together to form a dry rub and set aside.
2. Rub the canola oil all over the tenderloins and then coat them thoroughly with the dry rub. Set aside at room temperature while preheating your grill.
3. Preheat your grill over medium heat, or your oven to 400 degrees Fahrenheit.
4. Cook over the fire, while rotating occasionally, until somewhat charred and cooked until the centre of the thickest part of the pork reads approximately 145 degrees Fahrenheit on an internal meat thermometer (medium doneness), approximately 20 to 25 minutes. Or roast in the preheated oven for approximately the same time, checking for the same temperature doneness.
5. Let stand at room temperature for about 5 to 10 minutes before slicing to help retain juices.
6. Slice the tenderloins on a 45-degree angle for presentation. Arrange slices on a platter (or plate individually) and drizzle the chow chow sauce over top or serve it on the side.

Chorizo Sausage Meat

"Many times, it is hard to find raw chorizo sausages, so it is great to be able to make your own. Use this mix as is to put in recipes where ground meat is needed, or stuff into casings for sausages. If stuffing into casings, please use ground pork with more fat in it rather than less."

500g ground pork
2 tablespoons sweet smoked paprika
2 tablespoons apple cider vinegar
1 tablespoon granulated garlic or garlic powder
2 teaspoons salt
1 teaspoon dried oregano
1 teaspoon ground coriander
1 teaspoon ground cumin
1/2 – 1 teaspoon ground cayenne
1/2 teaspoon pepper
1/4 teaspoon ground cinnamon
1/4 teaspoon ground cloves

1. Mix all ingredients together.

Makes 500g of raw chorizo sausage meat

Egg & Chorizo Taco Filling

"A great way to incorporate nutritious eggs into Taco Night! Use this filling for any Mexican meal applications, such as tacos, burritos, quesadillas, etc. Everything you need in one pan – just scoop, fill, and serve!"

1 tablespoon canola oil
1 recipe of raw chorizo sausage meat (see above recipe)
6 large eggs, beaten
175g aged white cheddar, grated, about 1.5 cups
1/2 cup small diced yellow bell pepper
1/2 cup small diced tomatoes
1/2 cup small diced red onion, rinsed and drained for milder flavour

1 large jalapeno, seeds & membrane removed if desired, diced very small
1 small handful fresh cilantro, chopped
1/2 lime
Taco shells or tortillas, depending on the application
Serve with salsa and sour cream, if desired

1. In a medium non-stick pan on medium-high heat, add the oil and the chorizo. Cook until browned, approximately 10 minutes, while breaking up into small pieces with a wooden spoon.
2. Stir in the eggs and cook while stirring constantly until the eggs are fully cooked and combined with the chorizo, approximately 2 minutes.
3. Turn off the heat and stir in the grated cheese so it can melt.
4. Then evenly top this cooked mixture with the bell pepper, tomatoes, red onion, jalapeno sand cilantro. Squeeze the 1/2 lime over the mixture and serve immediately to fill taco shells or tortillas.

Makes 6 cups of filling, or up to 8 - 12 servings

Grilled Pork Chops with Apple Slaw – 6 servings

1/4 cup salt
4 cups cold water
6 bone-in pork chops
1 to 2 tablespoons canola oil
Salt & pepper
<u>Apple Slaw</u>
4 cups grated Gala apple (approx. 3 to 4 cored apples)
3 tablespoons apple cider vinegar
2 cups shredded purple cabbage
2 cups shredded green cabbage
1/2 cup grated carrot
1 cup mayonnaise
1/2 cup sour cream
3 tablespoons liquid honey
2 tablespoons grainy mustard
1.5 teaspoons seasoning salt
Freshly cracked pepper to taste

1. In a large bowl, dissolve the 1/4 cup salt in the water by whisking vigorously. Submerse the pork chops in this brine. Cover and refrigerate for 1 hour.
2. While the pork is brining, prepare the slaw by putting the grated apple in a large bowl and tossing with the vinegar to help prevent oxidization (going brown). Add the purple cabbage, green cabbage, carrot, mayonnaise, sour cream, honey, mustard, seasoning salt, and pepper. Toss to mix thoroughly and keep refrigerated.
3. When the pork has finished brining, remove the chops from the brine and pat them dry with paper towel. Preheat your BBQ over high heat until hot. Coat the chops with canola oil and seasoned them lightly with salt and pepper (remember that they will already be seasoned with salt from the brine).
4. When your BBQ is hot, place the chops on the grill and turn the heat down to medium-high. Grill the chops for approximately 5 to 8 minutes per side until just cooked – touching them should feel

somewhat firm, but not too firm (overcooked). Minimum internal temperature should be 150 degrees Fahrenheit.

5. Serve the chops topped with the apple slaw, or on the side, but this recipe shines when both are eaten together in the same bite.

Sausage, Tomato & Herb Frittata - Makes 8 to 12 Portions

2 tablespoons extra virgin olive oil
500g mild Italian sausages, removed from casings
1 medium onion, diced small
6 garlic cloves, minced
1 cup oil packed sundried tomatoes, drained and finely chopped
1/4 cup finely chopped fresh basil
1/4 cup finely chopped fresh oregano
2 teaspoons salt
1/2 teaspoon pepper
12 large eggs
1.25 cups grated Parmigiano Reggiano
Sour cream, optional

1. Preheat the oven to 350 degrees Fahrenheit and prepare a 10-inch round baking dish by spraying it with baking spray.
2. Add olive oil, sausage meat, onion and garlic to a frying pan and cook over medium heat for approximately 10 to 15 minutes until the sausage meat is cooked and the onion and garlic are soft. Stir occasionally breaking up the sausage meat into small bits as it cooks.
3. Transfer cooked sausage mixture to a large mixing bowl. Add the sundried tomatoes, basil, oregano, salt, pepper, eggs, and 3/4 cup of the grated parmesan cheese. Combine thoroughly together.
4. Pour the mixture into the prepared pan and take care to spread evenly. Top evenly with the remaining 1/2 cup of parmesan cheese. Bake for approximately 45 to 50 minutes until firm and lightly browned. The center of the frittata should not jiggle.
5. Remove from the oven and let stand on a cooling rack for at least 15 minutes before cutting and serving. Optional: serve with dollops of sour cream.

Sausages & Peppers in Buns – Makes 8 portions

"Why eat hot dogs when you can have these instead? You can also substitute steps #1 and #2 by cooking the sausages over charcoal instead (cook on a barbecue grid and eliminate the water in the recipe) – and if so, use the 1 tbsp of oil to start the cooking process of the onion in step #3."

8 Italian sausages
1 cup water
1 tbsp canola or vegetable oil
1 medium onion, cut in strips
2 red bell peppers, cut in strips
2 yellow bell peppers, cut in strips
2 tbsp fennel seed
1/4 cup beer or white wine
1 1/2 tsp salt
1 tsp sugar
1/2 tsp pepper
8 hot dog or hoagie type buns
Mayonnaise

1. Place sausages in a large pan with 1 cup of water. Cover and cook on medium-high heat for 10 minutes, timing from when the water starts boiling.
2. Remove the lid and continue cooking until the water has evaporated. When the water is gone and the 1 tbsp of oil and continue to cook the sausages until browned and cooked through, approximately 10 minutes. Remove the sausages and set aside.
3. Add the onion to the pan and cook until browned, stirring occasionally, approximately 5 minutes.
4. Add the peppers, fennel, 1/4 cup beer or wine, salt, sugar, and pepper. Stir and continue to cook, stirring occasionally, for 10 more minutes until peppers have become soft.
5. Add the reserved sausages and any residual liquid from the sitting sausages and cook for another 2 minutes.
6. Serve in buns with mayonnaise.

Toad In The Hole

"A classic British dish. Basically, a big Yorkshire pudding with sausages in it...with a funny name! Traditionally served with red onion gravy (see the Sauces chapter in this book), but I also like this served with maple syrup instead of the gravy. Good for breakfast, lunch, or dinner — you choose!"

1 tablespoon canola oil
5 sausages, 100g each (I use Bangers)
4 eggs, beaten
1.5 cups milk
1.5 cups all-purpose flour
4 tablespoons sugar
1.5 teaspoons salt

1. Preheat oven to 425 degrees Fahrenheit.
2. Add the oil to an 8x11-inch baking dish. Add the sausages to the baking dish and rotate them in the oil and use the sausages to spread the oil all over the bottom of the baking dish.
3. Bake the sausages for 10 minutes, turning them once at the 5-minute mark.
4. Meanwhile whisk the eggs and the milk together. Add the flour, sugar, and salt and continue whisking until fully combined.
5. After the sausages have baked for 10 minutes, quickly pour this batter in the baking dish with the sausages and get it back in the oven (making sure that the sausages are evenly spaced.
6. Bake for 30 minutes until golden brown and puffed up. Do not open the oven during the baking process or it will deflate.
7. Serve immediately at the table. It will deflate as it sits (this is normal).
8. Serve with drizzles of maple syrup OR red onion gravy (recipe below).

Makes 10 small portions

Slow-Cooker Pulled Pork

"First and foremost: nothing beats authentic pulled pork made with charcoal and wood, but if you don't have a smoker, then this your next best bet. Great pulled pork sandwiches in the ease of a slow-cooker. Serve on buns topped with coleslaw and your favourite mustard and BBQ Sauce."

2kg to 2.5kg boneless pork butt roast (pork shoulder roast)
2 tablespoons canola oil
Salt & pepper

1 medium onion, sliced
8 garlic cloves, chopped
1/2 cup brown sugar (not golden sugar)
2 tablespoons chilli powder
1 tablespoon liquid smoke
4 teaspoons salt
1 teaspoon pepper
1/2 cup beef broth

1/3 cup brown sugar (not golden sugar)
1 tablespoon white vinegar
1 teaspoon salt, or to taste
3 tablespoons cornstarch dissolved in 3 tablespoons beef broth or red wine

1. Cut the pork roast into 5 or 6 equal sized chunks. Coat with the canola oil and season with salt & pepper. Heat a pan over medium-high heat and once hot sear the chunks of pork until browned on all sides. Make sure you do not crowd the pan, or they won't brown as well. As each chunk is seared, place in slow-cooker.
2. While the pork chunks are searing, add the onion, garlic, 1/2 cup brown sugar, chilli powder, liquid smoke, 4 tsp salt, and 1 tsp pepper to the slow-cooker.
3. When the pork is done searing and all chunks are now in the slow-cooker, carefully add the beef broth to the pan and stir to deglaze (remove the browned bits off the pan into the liquid). Now add this broth to the slow-cooker as well.

4. Put the lid on the slow cooker and turn on low. Cook for 8 to 9 hours.
5. Once cooked, remove the chunks of pork from the liquid. Shred each piece of pork with 2 forks and set aside in a covered large bowl to keep warm.
6. Pour the liquid (and chunks of onion and garlic) into a pot. Puree with a hand immersion blender (or place in a food processor or blender to puree smooth, and then into a pot). Stir in the 1/3 cup brown sugar, white vinegar, salt, and the dissolved cornstarch mixture. Bring to a boil to thicken. Mix in 3 cups of this thickened sauce to the shredded pork. (keep leftover sauce to serve as extra dipping sauce if desired)
7. Serve on buns topped with coleslaw and your favourite mustard.

Makes approximately 8 cups of pulled pork

RECIPE NOTES

POULTRY

Boneless Turkey Roast – Makes 6 – 8 portions

"A turkey thigh wrapped up in a turkey breast will please all turkey lovers.

1 boneless skin-on turkey breast, approximately 1kg
Salt & pepper
2 tablespoons minced onion
2 tablespoons chopped fresh sage
2 garlic cloves, minced
1 boneless turkey thigh, approximately 350g
6 to 8 strips of bacon

1. Preheat oven to 325 degrees Fahrenheit.
2. Cut the thickest part of the breast in half (without cutting all the way through) to make the breast more consistent in thickness (butterfly cut) and allow the breast to spread out more (have more surface area).
3. With the skin-side down, season with salt and pepper, and evenly scatter the onion, sage, and garlic over the breast.
4. Remove and discard the skin from the thigh. Lay the thigh on the seasoned breast and then season the thigh with more salt & pepper.
5. Starting with the end of the breast, roll up the thigh inside the breast meat to form a football shape, tucking in the parts of the breast that may be sticking out. Season the top of the breast skin with more salt and pepper.
6. Lay strips of the bacon lengthwise, side by side, on the top of the roast until it is covered. Carefully tie butcher's twine every two inches in the opposite direction of the bacon strips, to secure the roast. Then tie one more piece of butcher's twine lengthwise around the roast (the same direction of the bacon strips).
7. Place the tied roast on a rack in a roasting pan and insert an oven proof thermometer. Roast in the oven for approximately 30 minutes per pound until the internal temperature reaches 165 degrees Fahrenheit, approximately 1 hour and 45 minutes.
8. Remove from the oven, carefully remove the butcher's twine, and let rest for at least 10 minutes before carving. Serve with your favourite cranberry sauce and enjoy!

4-Hour Turkey Gravy

"Don't be intimidated by the name – it's 4 hours of cooking time, not 4 hours of constant attention, and you have to cook a turkey in this time anyway. Made from the slow caramelization process of vegetables. This gravy offers tons of flavour and is well worth the effort"

2 medium carrots, sliced into 1/4 inch coins
2 celery stalks, sliced 1/4 inch
3 tablespoons canola oil or vegetable oil, divided
1 medium onion, sliced thin
1/4 cup butter
6 tablespoons flour
1/2 cup white wine
2 cups total of chicken broth and reserved roasted turkey drippings combined
Extra broth, if desired
1 teaspoon sugar
Salt & pepper to taste

1. Add carrot, celery and 2 tablespoons of the oil to a large heavy bottomed non-stick pan. Toss to coat in the oil and cook over low to medium-low heat for approximately 1.5 hours, stirring occasionally. The carrot and celery will shrink in size, become soft, and just start to caramelize. *DO NOT CROWD THE PAN – It is important to use a large enough pan otherwise the vegetables will just steam in their juices instead of caramelizing. The secret is to slowly caramelize the vegetables without burning them.
2. Stir in the onion and the other tablespoon of oil to the carrots and celery and continue to cook, stirring occasionally, for another approximate 1.5 hours – all of the vegetables will become almost all dark brown (caramelized).
3. Add the butter to the vegetables, let it melt, and stir in the flour. Cook for 45 more minutes, stirring occasionally. The flour will become "nut brown" in colour.
4. Stir in the wine slowly. It will start to get extremely thick. Continue by slowly stirring in the broth while incorporating to ensure no lumps.

5. Increase the heat to medium or medium-high while stirring to bring to a boil. Boiling will activate the full thickening power of the flour.
6. Strain the mixture through a wire-mesh strainer while pushing as much liquid as possible from the cooked vegetables. Discard the cooked vegetables.
7. Season the gravy with the sugar, salt, and pepper. If it is too thick then add a bit more liquid broth if desired.

Makes approximately 1.75 cups

Orange Balsamic Poultry Glaze
"Great on chicken or duck"

1/2 cup orange marmalade
1/2 cup orange juice
1/2 cup balsamic vinegar
2 tablespoons soy sauce
2 tablespoons liquid honey
2 sprigs fresh rosemary

1. Combine the marmalade, orange juice, balsamic vinegar, soy sauce, and honey in a small pot. Add the rosemary sprigs.
2. Bring to a boil and reduce uncovered until about 1/3 or 1/4 of the volume is left in the pot, approximately 1/2 cup.
3. Discard the rosemary sprigs.
4. Use as a basting glaze while roasting chicken or duck (whole birds or cut into pieces).

Makes approximately 1/2 cup of glaze – enough for 1 chicken or duck

Chicken Marbella – Makes 8 – 10 portions

"An incredible sheet-pan meal that pairs chicken legs with prunes, olives and capers. The sweetness of the prunes contrasts perfectly with the brininess of the olives and capers. Marinate in a large bag, dump onto a sheet pan and bake - easy! Makes an amazing presentation on a platter at the table."

8-10 bone-in skin-on whole chicken legs (drumstick & thigh together)
30 pitted prunes
8 garlic cloves, crushed
4 bay leaves
1 cup pitted green olives
1/2 packed cup of fresh oregano leaves
1/2 cup white wine
100ml bottle of capers, not drained
1/4 cup extra virgin olive oil
1/4 cup red wine vinegar
1/4 cup molasses
2 teaspoons salt
1 teaspoon pepper

1. Make about 5 cuts in each chicken leg (scored through the skin and into the flesh a bit) to help marinate the chicken more.
2. Place all the ingredients in an extra-large zippered plastic bag. Seal and toss to mix up all the ingredients and to coat the chicken. Place in the refrigerator for 24 to 48 hours, flipping the bag over a few times per day to help marinate the chicken evenly. Alternatively, instead of using a plastic bag, a covered large bowl or container will work, removing the lid and mixing up a few times per day.
3. Heat oven to 400 degrees Fahrenheit. Empty the entire contents onto a 12x18 inch sheet-pan, arranging the chicken skin side up and all the prunes and olives in between the chicken pieces. Bake for approximately 50 minutes, basting 2 or 3 times during the cooking process, until the chicken is done by reaching an internal temperature of at least 160 degrees Fahrenheit or 71 degrees Celsius.
4. Arrange the chicken legs on a platter and garnish with the remain sheet-pan ingredients (prunes, olives, capers, etc.) and most of the

liquid. Give the chicken a small sprinkling of salt and serve immediately.

Turkey Meatloaf with Cranberry Glaze – Makes 1 loaf

Glaze/Topping
1 – 340g bag of fresh cranberries (or thawed from frozen)
3/4 cup dark brown sugar
1/2 cup ketchup
1/4 teaspoon salt
Meatloaf
1.5 pounds (681g) ground turkey thigh (or regular ground turkey)
1 cup fine breadcrumbs
3/4 cup minced onion
3 large eggs
3 garlic cloves, minced
1 tablespoon salt
2 teaspoons ground dry sage
1/2 teaspoon pepper

1. Preheat the oven to 350 degrees Fahrenheit and prepare a standard size bread loaf pan by lining it with parchment paper (make sure there is enough of the parchment paper sticking out of the pan for easy extraction of the whole loaf when cooked).
2. In a heavy bottomed medium size pot, add all of the ingredients for the Glaze/Topping. Turn heat to medium-high and cook stirring frequently while also mashing with a potato masher as the berries cook and break down, until a smooth thick consistency is reached, approximately 15 minutes.
3. Add all of the meatloaf ingredients to a large bowl and mix thoroughly. Press into the prepared loaf pan and cover with the cranberry topping. Bake for approximately 1 to 1.25 hours until the internal temperature of the meat loaf has reached a minimum of 160 degrees Fahrenheit (or 71 degrees Celsius). Let rest for at least 15 minutes before extracting from the pan. Slice and serve immediately.

Roasted Stuffed Turkey

"Over the years I have instructed countless people verbally on how to stuff and roast a whole turkey – now I have it in written form for you"

1 pound (454g) mild Italian sausages, casings removed
1 medium onion, diced small
4 garlic cloves, minced
2 tablespoons dried sage
Salt and pepper to season
454g (1 pound) loaf regular sized sandwich bread, cut in cubes
1 large egg, beaten
1 cup chicken broth/stock
1/2 cup dried cranberries
1 medium apple, diced small
7kg (15.5 pound) whole turkey
6 bacon slices
1/2 cup mayonnaise
Seasoning salt
Aluminum foil
4-Hour Turkey Gravy recipe (in this chapter)

1. Preheat oven to 325 degrees Fahrenheit.
2. In a pan over medium heat, combine the sausage meat, onion, garlic, sage, and sprinkle with some salt and pepper. Stir while cooking to break the sausage meat into small chunks until the meat is thoroughly cooked, approximately 8-10 minutes. Add to the bread cubes in a large mixing bowl.
3. Combine the egg and chicken broth/stock together and evenly pour over the bread cube mixture. Evenly toss in the dried cranberries and diced apple until everything is thoroughly mixed together, and season to taste with salt and pepper (for food safe reasons, the sample you are going to taste can be cooked first because of the raw egg in the mixture. Simply place a small portion in a microwavable dish and heat thoroughly before consuming).
4. Prepare the turkey by placing it on a rack (breast side up) in a roasting pan. Carefully separate the skin from the breast meat so that you have

2 "pockets" on each side where you can slide the bacon slices into (3 slices on each side) between the skin and the breast meat. Try to make sure that the bacon slices are covering as much of the breast meat as possible as this will help to keep that breast meat moist.

5. Stuff the turkey with the prepared and seasoned stuffing mixture. Slather the top and the sides (in all the crevices too) of the turkey with the mayonnaise. Sprinkle liberally with seasoning salt.

6. Wrap and seal the roasting pan tight with aluminum foil (this will trap steam and help to keep the turkey moist without having to baste it) and roast in the oven for 3 hours.

7. After 3 hours, remove the foil and reserve the foil for covering the turkey when it is resting when done. Carefully extract the juices on the bottom of the roasting pan to a measuring cup (a turkey baster is a good tool for this – just tip the pan a bit to create a depth of juices for sucking out with the baster). Let these juices stand to separate the fat while the turkey finishes cooking. Once separated, discard the fat from the top and add the juice (drippings) to your gravy – see Turkey Gravy Recipe in this chapter.

8. Place the turkey back in the oven (uncovered) for approximately 1 more hour until browned <u>and</u> a thermometer in the thickest part of the thigh reads 180 degrees Fahrenheit. Cover the turkey with the reserved foil and let it rest for at least 30 minutes before removing the stuffing and then carving the turkey (carve with the bacon slices in place). Serve immediately.

Makes 1 whole Stuffed Turkey

Marinated Chicken with Garlic Quinoa

"If you want to use fresh herbs in the marinade instead of the dried herbs, chop them fine and use 3 tablespoons chopped oregano and 3 tablespoons chopped basil. Cooking the quinoa uncovered (instead of covered) will result in more texture and flavour."

2/3 cup olive oil
1/3 cup fresh lemon juice, zest from the lemons reserved
1 tablespoon white wine vinegar
6 garlic cloves, crushed
1 tablespoon dried oregano leaves
1 tablespoon dried basil leaves
Salt and pepper to season
6 boneless/skinless chicken breast halves
2 tablespoons canola oil
6 garlic cloves, chopped
2 cups quinoa
4 cups water
1 teaspoon salt
1/2 teaspoon pepper

1. Mix the olive oil, lemon juice, vinegar, 6 crushed garlic, oregano, and basil in a large bowl. Season to taste with salt & pepper – season it as if you were making a salad dressing.
2. Add the chicken and marinate in fridge for 3 - 4 hours, tossing occasionally.
3. Remove the chicken from the marinade and grill over a medium to medium-high heat until done, approximately 20 minutes depending on the temperature of your grill. Alternatively, bake in a 400-degree oven for approximately 20 minutes. Internal temperature of the chicken should be a minimum of 72 degrees Celsius or 165 degrees Fahrenheit.
4. While the chicken is cooking prepare the quinoa – add the canola oil and chopped 6 cloves of garlic to a pot and cook briefly over medium heat – make sure to not burn the garlic otherwise it will taste bitter. Stir in the dry quinoa and cook for another 30 seconds. Add the water, 1 teaspoon salt and 1/2 teaspoon pepper and continue to cook on medium to medium-high heat <u>uncovered</u>, stirring occasionally, until all

of the liquid has been absorbed/evaporated, approximately 15 to 20 minutes. Re-season to taste if necessary.

5. Serve a mound of quinoa topped with the chicken breast, and garnish with the reserved lemon zest.

Makes 6 servings

RECIPE NOTES

SEAFOOD

Fillets of Sole Meuniere

"Pronounced 'mun yair', this is a classic fish preparation"

Canola oil
4 to 6 sole fillets (approximately 60g each)
Salt & pepper
Flour
Juice of a lemon, approx. 2 tablespoons
1/4 cup chopped fresh parsley
5 tablespoons cold butter

1. Heat a non-stick pan over medium-high heat.
2. While heating, season the fillets with salt & pepper, then dredge in flour.
3. Add approximately 1 tbsp canola oil to the pan and then add the fillets to the pan, presentation side down first. Sauté until lightly browned. Turn over carefully with a spatula and brown the other side.
4. Transfer the fillets to plates and squeeze the lemon over them. Sprinkle with parsley.
5. Add the butter to the hot pan and swirl until foaming brown to make browned butter and immediately pour it over the fish.

Makes 4 to 6 portions

Shrimp Enchiladas

"The heat in this dish is solely from the canned chipotle peppers — for less spiciness only use 1 chipotle pepper divided, instead of 2"

7 teaspoons canola oil or grapeseed oil, divided
10 small 4-inch flour tortillas
1/2 cup minced shallots, divided
2 chipotle peppers (from a can)*, divided, & minced
340g raw small prawns, no shells
1 teaspoon salt, divided
1/2 teaspoon pepper, divided
1/4 cup whipping cream
1 – 796ml can of diced tomatoes, divided
1 teaspoon sugar
170g Monterey Jack cheese, sliced or grated
Sour cream & sliced green onions as garnish

1. Preheat oven to 375 degrees and with a small pastry brush spread 1 teaspoon of the oil in a 9x13 baking dish. Lay the 10 small flour tortillas out on the counter or on a baking sheet.
2. Heat a pan over med/high heat. Add 3 teaspoons of oil, 1/4 cup shallots, 1 minced chipotle pepper, shrimp, 1/2 teaspoon of the salt, 1/4 teaspoon of the pepper, the whipping cream, and 1/2 cup of the diced tomatoes. Cook while stirring until the shrimp are just barely cooked through, approximately 3 to 4 minutes. Distribute this shrimp mixture with a slotted spoon evenly on the tortillas. Roll up each tortilla and place them seam side down into the prepared 9x13 baking dish.
3. Boil the remaining sauce in the pan until thick and then spoon over the rolled tortillas.
4. Return the pan to the heat. Add the other 3 teaspoons of oil, 1/4 cup shallots, and 1 minced chipotle pepper and sauté for 1 minute. Add the remaining diced tomatoes, 1/2 teaspoon salt, 1/4 teaspoon pepper, and the sugar. Cook until thickened. Spoon over the rolled enchiladas and top with the cheese.

5. Bake for 15 to 20 minutes until the cheese melts and turns lightly golden. Garnish with the sour cream and green onions and serve immediately.

Makes 10 small enchiladas

*You can usually find small cans of chipotle peppers in adobo sauce in the Mexican section of major grocery stores.

Simple Maple Chili Glaze for Salmon

"Simple: just 4 ingredients but tastes great! I came up with this recipe at the 2019 EGGtoberfest for Big Green Egg in Atlanta GA. People kept asking me for the recipe, so here it is."

1/2 cup maple syrup
2 tablespoons soy sauce
1 teaspoon sesame oil
1/2 teaspoon ground cayenne
Garnish with angle cut green onions, optional

1. Mix everything together. Glaze a bit onto salmon when in the last stages of the cooking process. Pour the remining glaze over the salmon when serving or serve it in dipping cups.

West Coast Cauliflower Kedgeree

"A Kedgeree is a curried rice dish from the UK and is classically made with smoked haddock and boiled eggs. We have replaced the traditional rice, with cauliflower rice and smoked salmon instead of the haddock."

4 large BC eggs, hardboiled, cooled
1 large head of cauliflower
2 tablespoons of avocado oil, or canola oil
1 medium onion, diced small
3 cloves of garlic, minced
2 teaspoons grated fresh ginger
3 teaspoons curry powder
2 teaspoons salt
1 teaspoon ground turmeric
1/2 teaspoon ground pepper
1 cup frozen peas
175 grams smoked salmon, broken into bite sized chunks
Chopped fresh parsley, for garnish
Lemon wedges, for serving

1. Peel the hardboiled eggs and cut them into quarters. Set aside.
2. Rice the cauliflower by grating the florets with a cheese grater, or by pulsing in a food processor to transform into rice looking granules, about 6 cups. Set aside.
3. Heat a large skillet over medium heat. Add the oil, then the onion, garlic, ginger, curry powder, salt, turmeric and pepper. Stir to combine and cook until soft and fragrant, approximately 2 to 3 minutes, stirring occasionally.
4. Stir in the frozen peas and cook for another minute.
5. Turn the heat to medium-high and add the reserved cauliflower rice from step 2. Cook while stirring constantly for approximately 3 to 4 minutes. It is important to use a large skillet over higher heat so that the cauliflower granules stay more separate and don't become mushy (the larger pan and higher heat will evaporate any moisture that comes out of the cauliflower).

6. Turn off the heat and stir in the chunks of smoked salmon. Portion into dishes while garnishing equally with the quartered eggs and some parsley. Serve with lemon wedges.

Makes 7 cups

SIDE DISHES

Cheese Baked Mashed Potatoes

"A classic Scottish side dish called Rumbledethumps"

4 extra-large russet potatoes, peeled and diced one-half inch
5 cups shredded (or thinly sliced) green cabbage
1 small onion, diced small
6 large cloves of garlic, minced
3/4 cup butter
4 teaspoons salt
1 teaspoon pepper
3/4 cup whipping cream
1 cup grated aged cheddar
Fresh chopped parsley, for garnish

1. Steam the diced potatoes over boiling water until tender, approximately 20 minutes.
2. Preheat the oven to 350 degrees.
3. While the potatoes are steaming, melt 1/4 cup of the butter in a large pan over medium heat until it just starts foaming. Add the cabbage, onion, garlic and 1 easpoon of the salt to the pan and cook until mostly soft, while stirring occasionally. Approximately 15 minutes.
4. Cube the remaining 1/2 cup butter and add it to the steamed potatoes along with the other 3 teaspoons salt and the 1 teaspoon pepper. Mash until thoroughly combined.
5. Stir the cabbage mixture, whipping cream, and 1/2 cup of the grated cheddar into the potatoes until thoroughly combined. Taste and re-season if necessary.
6. Transfer to a baking dish, top with the remaining 1/2 cup cheddar and parsley, and bake for 20 minutes.

Makes approximately 6 to 10 side portions

Chickpea Curry in a Hurry

"My version of a quick chickpea curry. A great vegetarian meal or stir in cubes of cooked chicken at the end."

2 tbsp canola oil
1 small onion, diced small
1 carrot, cut into quarters lengthwise and sliced thin
1 celery stalk, cut in half lengthwise and sliced thin
4 garlic cloves, minced
2 tablespoons dark brown sugar
1 tablespoon salt
1 tablespoon curry powder
2 teaspoons garam masala*
1 teaspoon turmeric
1/2 teaspoon pepper
1 – 540ml can chickpeas, drained, reserving 2 tablespoons of the liquid
1 red bell pepper, diced small
1 – 398ml can coconut milk
1 teaspoon vegetable stock paste*
2 tablespoons cornstarch dissolved in the reserved chickpea liquid
Garnish with plain yogurt, currants, and chopped cilantro

1. Heat a large pan slightly over medium heat. Add the oil, onion, carrot, celery, garlic, sugar, salt, curry powder, garam masala, turmeric, and pepper. Mix together and cook for approximately 5 minutes, stirring occasionally, until vegetables are soft and the mixture becomes thick.
2. Add the drained chick peas, bell pepper, coconut milk, vegetable paste, and dissolved cornstarch mixture. Heat to a boil while stirring to thicken.
3. Serve immediately garnished with plain yogurt, currants, and cilantro

Makes approximately 6 side-dish servings

*Garam masala is a blend of spices used extensively in Indian cuisine. Most major grocery stores have this in either their spices section or the imported foods aisle.

*Vegetable stock paste is vegetable broth that has been reduced down to a concentrated paste form. The most common brand found at your local grocery stores is "Better Than Bouillon" Vegetable Base – in small glass jars. Once opened this will last 1 year easily in your refrigerator.

Butternut Mash

"What a wonderful change to mashed potatoes, especially in the fall – very autumnal!"

1.36kg (3 pounds) butternut squash
1.5 tbsp brown sugar
2 tsp salt
1/4 tsp pepper

1. Peel the butter nut squash and cut the flesh into 1/2 inch cubes, discarding the seeds.
2. Steam for approximately 20 minutes until tender.
3. Mash with the sugar, salt, & pepper until smooth. Scoop into a wire mesh strainer to let drain for approximately 10 minutes before serving (this will help the mashed squash to have a firmer texture).

Flambéed Mushrooms — Makes 4 side portions

"One of the easiest side dishes, or steak toppers, you will ever make — and a showy one at the stove or side burner of your BBQ! Using a peatier scotch (single malts from the Islay region) will produce more residual flavours."

2 tablespoons canola oil
1 pound (454g) button mushrooms, quartered
1/2 teaspoon dried thyme
Salt & pepper
1 to 2 tablespoons Scotch whiskey

1. Heat a medium pan over medium-high heat.
2. Add the oil, then the mushrooms, thyme, and season with salt & pepper. Sauté until the mushrooms have shrunk in size and they start to turn brown, approximately 5 to 7 minutes, stirring occasionally.
3. Remove the pan from the heat to let cool slightly, approximately 30 seconds. Carefully add the whiskey and carefully ignite with a long match/lighter. Flambé until the flames subside.
4. Re-season with salt & pepper if necessary and serve immediately as a side dish or on top of steak.

Oven Roasted Root Vegetables — Makes 5 – 6 cups

"To prevent excessive bleeding of the red beets into the other vegetables, soak and rinse the diced beets with cold water and then drain thoroughly before using in the recipe"

<u>1 heaping cup of 1/2 inch diced of each of the following root vegetables:</u>
Onion
Rutabaga
Turnip
Sweet Potato
Beets
Carrots

2 large sprigs of fresh rosemary
2 tablespoons canola oil, vegetable oil, or olive oil

2 teaspoons salt
1/2 teaspoon pepper
1 tablespoon Maple Syrup

1. Preheat oven to 450 degrees Fahrenheit.
2. In a large bowl toss all of the ingredients together (except for the maple syrup).
3. Spread on a large baking sheet making sure the cut vegetables are not crowded (if they are crowded do them on 2 smaller baking sheets and switch your oven to convection).
4. Bake for 30 minutes, tossing every 5 to 7 minutes.
5. Add the maple syrup and stir to coat. Bake for another 10 minutes.

Rosemary Garlic Quinoa – Makes approximately 6 servings

"Quinoa (pronounced 'keen-wah') is superior to other grains because it is a complete protein, containing 8 essential amino acids. It is actually a seed, not a grain, and is gluten free. It is highly appreciated for its nutritional value, as its protein content is very high. Unlike wheat or rice (which are low in lysine), quinoa contains a balanced set of essential amino acids."

2 tablespoons canola oil
6 garlic cloves, chopped
2 tablespoons chopped fresh rosemary
2 cups quinoa
4 cups water
1 teaspoon salt
1/2 teaspoon pepper

1. Add the canola oil, chopped garlic and rosemary to a pot and cook briefly over medium heat – make sure to not burn the garlic otherwise it will taste bitter. Stir in the quinoa and cook for another 30 seconds. Add the water, salt & pepper and continue to cook on medium to medium-high heat uncovered, stirring occasionally, until all of the liquid has been absorbed/evaporated, approximately 15 to 20 minutes. Re-season to taste if necessary.

Rosemary Roasted Potatoes

2 pounds baby new potatoes
5 tablespoons olive oil
4 stalks of fresh rosemary or 2 tablespoons dry rosemary
6 whole cloves of garlic peeled
Salt and fresh cracked pepper to taste

1. Pre-heat oven to 450 degrees.
2. Wash and dry potatoes, cutting larger ones in half to allow for even cooking. Place them in a bowl with garlic cloves.
3. Drizzle with olive oil.
4. Strip rosemary from stalks and sprinkle over potatoes.
5. Season generously with salt and fresh cracked pepper.
6. Toss to coat.
7. Place on a cookie sheet and bake for approximately 25-30 minutes until fully cooked and browned, stirring half way through.

Smoky Stuffed Sweet Potatoes

"Orange fleshed sweet potatoes are packed full of nutrition just like eggs! Pairing them together with smoked gouda and sweet smoked paprika makes this dish extra delicious."

2 large orange sweet potatoes, approximately 800g each, baked and cooled
10 fresh spinach leaves, chopped
1/4 cup sliced sun-dried tomatoes, packed in oil, drained
1/2 cup finely grated smoked gouda, divided into 2 parts
4 large BC eggs
1.5 tablespoons milk
1.5 teaspoons sweet smoked paprika
1.5 teaspoons salt
1/2 teaspoon pepper

1. Preheat oven to 375 degrees.
2. Cut the cold sweet potatoes in half lengthwise and carefully scoop out the centers, leaving approximately a 1/2-inch border of sweet potato

left around the edges and bottoms. Be careful not to scoop all the way down to the skin otherwise your potato halves will not hold the egg mixture like a vessel. Placed them on a parchment lined baking sheet.

3. In each of the 4 prepared halves, divide and sprinkle equal amounts of the spinach, sun-dried tomatoes, and 1/4 cup of the smoked gouda.
4. In a medium bowl, whisk the eggs, milk, smoked paprika, salt, and pepper thoroughly together.
5. Carefully ladle this egg mixture into the prepared halves of sweet potato.
6. Sprinkle the remaining 1/4 cup smoked gouda over the filled halves.
7. Bake for 15 to 20 minutes until the egg mixture has set.
8. Turn the oven to broil, and place under the broiler until just browned a bit, 1 to 2 minutes.
9. Let cool for about 10 to 20 minutes before serving.

Makes 4 large portions

South-Western Creamed Corn

"Make sure you add the lime juice at the very end when the pan is off the heat. This keeps it tasting very fresh and lively."

3 strips of bacon, sliced into 1/4 inch pieces
3 tablespoons minced onion
1 chipotle pepper (from a can), minced
2 garlic cloves, minced
5 cups fresh corn kernels or 5 cups frozen (thawed & drained)
1 medium red bell pepper, diced small (approximately 1 cup)
1.5 teaspoons salt
1/4 teaspoons pepper
1 cup whipping cream
1 cup grated old cheddar
Juice of 1/2 lime

1. In a large pan over medium heat, cook the bacon pieces until cooked, but not crisp, approximately 5 minutes.
2. Add the onion, chipotle, and garlic. Stir and cook for 1 minute.
3. Add the corn, bell pepper, salt and pepper. Stir and cook for 2 to 3 minutes.
4. Stir in the cream and cheddar and continue cooking while stirring until thickened to desired consistency, approximately 3 to 4 more minutes.
5. Remove from the heat, stir in the fresh lime juice and serve immediately.

Makes approximately 7 cups

RECIPE NOTES

DESSERTS

Avocado Chocolate Mousse

"A perfect dessert for to offer your guests who don't eat gluten or dairy"

240g ripe avocado flesh (approximately 2 small avocados)
1/2 cup semi-sweet chocolate chips
6 tbsp coconut milk
3 tbsp sugar
1 tsp vanilla extract
1/8 tsp salt

1. Peel and pit the avocados and place the flesh in a food processor.
2. Melt the chocolate chips and add to the food processor.
3. Add the coconut milk, sugar, vanilla, and salt to the food processor and puree until smooth.
4. Portion into dessert dishes and chill in the refrigerator for a minimum of 2 to 3 hours.
5. Optional garnish idea: mint leaves and fresh raspberries.

Makes approximately 1.75 cups

Amaretto Truffles with Vanilla Pastry Cream

"This chocolate dessert is well worth the effort, even if your hands get a bit messy"

Truffles
1 cup semi-sweet chocolate chips
1/4 cup butter
2 tablespoons icing sugar, sifted
2 tablespoons cream cheese, room temperature
3 tablespoons amaretto
unsweetened cocoa powder
sliced almonds, crushed

1. In a double boiler, gently melt the chocolate and the butter together until smooth and fully combined.
2. Remove from the heat and stir in the icing sugar, then the cream cheese until fully combined and lump free.
3. Stir in the amaretto and chill in the refrigerator until solid (min. 2 hours).
4. Using a spoon, quickly scoop out a heaping teaspoon of the mixture, roll and press it into a ball in your hands, and then roll it in cocoa powder or almonds. Do each one individually and set aside before moving on to the next one, to help prevent melting of the chocolate.

Vanilla Pastry Cream
1 cup milk
1/4 cup white sugar
1 teaspoon vanilla extract
1/8 teaspoon salt
3 egg yolks
1 tablespoon flour, sifted
1.5 teaspoons cornstarch, sifted
More amaretto and fresh mint leaves for garnish

1. In a heavy bottomed pot, mix the milk, sugar, vanilla, and salt together and bring to a boil over medium-high heat, stirring frequently.

2. Beat the egg yolks with the flour and cornstarch until it becomes pale yellow.
3. Starting very slowly, gradually add the hot milk to the beaten yolks to ensure that the eggs don't get too hot all at once.
4. Return the mixture to the pot and bring to a boil over medium heat while whisking constantly, approximately 2 to 3 minutes. It is at the boiling point that the mixture will thicken. Spoon into a separate bowl and chill.

For each portion, place a dollop of pastry cream in a martini glass, and nestle 3 truffles in the pastry cream. Drizzle with a teaspoon of amaretto and garnish with a fresh mint leaf.

Makes Approximately 12 – 15 truffles (4 – 5 servings)

Blueberry Cheesecake Crêpes

"For breakfast or dessert – these crêpes are to die for!"

Cheesecake Filling & Cheesecake Sauce:

1 cup cream cheese
1/2 cup ricotta cheese
Zest of 1 lemon finely chopped
Juice of 1/2 lemon
1 teaspoon vanilla extract
1 cup icing sugar, sifted
3 cups blueberries

Stir the cream cheese until smooth and pliable. Stir in the ricotta. Add the lemon zest, lemon juice, vanilla and icing sugar. Blend until smooth.
Cheesecake Filling: use 1 cup of this cream cheese mixture combined with 2 cups of the blueberries.
Cheesecake Sauce: use the remaining cream cheese mixture combined with the 1 remaining cup of blueberries.
Refrigerate both bowls until thoroughly chilled.

Blueberry Topping:

2 cups fresh or frozen blueberries
1/3 cup granulated sugar
Juice of 1 lemon
2 tablespoons apple juice, or cold water
1.5 tablespoons cornstarch
Pinch nutmeg

Combine blueberries, sugar and lemon juice in a pot over medium/high heat. Mash berries a little while cooking, for approximately 3 - 4 minutes.
Combine apple juice (or water) and cornstarch together in a small bowl, and whisk into the boiling berry mixture. Stir until thick and remove from the heat.
Stir in nutmeg.

Crêpe Batter:

1/2 cup all-purpose flour
1/2 cup milk
1/4 cup lukewarm water
2 eggs
2 tablespoons melted butter
1.5 tablespoons white sugar
Pinch of salt

Butter for the pan

Combine all the batter ingredients. Mix until smooth – a blender or food processor works perfectly. Place the batter in a container suitable for pouring. Cover and allow to rest for half an hour, or refrigerate for up to 24 hours. Place a non-stick pan over medium heat and coat with a bit of butter. Stir the batter briefly. For each crêpe, pour about 2 - 3 tbsp of the batter into the hot pan – immediately lift the pan and start rolling the batter evenly over the pan surface. Cook until it is set and the bottom is golden before flipping it over to brown the other side.
Remove from the pan and continue cooking all your crepes- keep them stacked to keep warm.

To Assemble:

Spoon some of the cheesecake filling onto one side of a crêpe. Roll 1 to 3 of these crepes per portion.
Spoon some of the cheesecake sauce over the crêpes, and then top with the blueberry topping.
Garnish with more fresh blueberries, powdered sugar, and a mint leaf if desired.

Makes approximately 8 crêpes

Lemon Glazed Pound Cake

"Originating in Europe in the first half of the 18th century, this traditional loaf weighed 4 pounds, because of creating it with one pound of each of its four ingredients. Break out your kitchen scale for this one."

1-pound (454g) butter, room temperature
1-pound (454g) white sugar
1-pound (454g) eggs (approximately 8 to 9 large eggs)
2 teaspoons vanilla extract
1-pound (454g) all-purpose flour
1 teaspoon salt

Lemon Glaze
1 cup icing sugar
Zest of 1 lemon, finely chopped/grated
Juice of 1 lemon
1/4 teaspoon salt

1. Preheat oven to 350 degrees Fahrenheit. Prepare 2 standard loaf pans with baking spray or butter.
2. In a stand mixer, beat the butter and sugar together thoroughly on high speed until fluffy and pale, about 2 to 3 minutes, scraping down the bowl and paddle occasionally.
3. Put the eggs in a pourable container (like an extra-large measuring cup) along with the vanilla. Put the mixer on medium-low speed and pour in the eggs one at a time (estimate by one yolk at a time), gradually increase speed to medium until thoroughly combined, scraping down the bowl and paddle occasionally.
4. Mix the 1 teaspoon of salt into the flour. Gently fold in the flour mixture 1/2 at a time until just combined. Do not overmix.
5. Scoop batter evenly into the 2 prepared loaf pans and smooth the batter with a spatula.
6. Bake for approximately 50 to 60 minutes until an inserted toothpick comes out clean. Let cool in the pans for about 5 to 10 minutes, before removing from the pans and transferring to a cooling rack.

7. Once the cakes are room temperature, in a small bowl mix the icing sugar, zest, lemon juice, and 1/4 teaspoon of salt together and pour evenly over the loafs. Slice and serve.

Makes 2 loaf pans of cake

Mocha Rum Chocolate Soufflés

"Soufflés are not as difficult as some people think, and this makes a wonderful dessert. Baking time will depend on the temperature of your raw eggs. The finished soufflés will deflate a bit as they sit, but this is normal."

Butter for ramekins
5 ounces (142g) semi-sweet baking chocolate
2 tablespoons dark rum
1 tablespoon instant coffee powder
1/4 teaspoon salt
6 tablespoons sugar, plus more for dusting ramekins
6 large eggs, yolks separated from whites
Fresh raspberries (or thawed from frozen), for serving
Whipped cream, for serving

1. Preheat oven to 375 degrees Fahrenheit.
2. Prepare four 1-cup sized (250ml) oven safe ramekins by buttering them and then dusting them with sugar thoroughly, tapping out any excess sugar.
3. Chop the chocolate into small bits. Alternatively, instead of chopping, you can use 5 ounces of pure semi-sweet chocolate chips instead of the squares of baking chocolate.
4. Place a medium pot half filled with water on the stove and maintain a low simmer.
5. In a stainless-steel bowl (that is big enough to sit on the pot without touching the water), place the prepared chocolate, rum, instant coffee, salt, and 3 tablespoons of the sugar. Let this mixture slowly melt together by sitting over the simmering water until just melted (do not heat longer than necessary) and then stir to combine. Remove the bowl from the heat and stir in the egg yolks, one at a time, to this chocolate mixture.
6. Beat the egg whites in a stand mixture with whisk attachment until foamy, then add the remaining 3 tablespoons of sugar. With the sugar added, beat the egg whites on high speed until stiff peaks form. Stir approximately 1/3 of these whipped egg whites into the chocolate mixture. Gently fold in the remaining egg whites thoroughly.

7. Pour the soufflé mixture equally into the prepared ramekins. Once filled, tap them on the counter a few times to knock out any air bubbles. Place the filled ramekins on a baking sheet and bake in the oven for approximately 17 to 20 minutes (depending on the temperature of your eggs), until puffed up, set and cracked on top.

8. Put each hot ramekin on a serving plate and top with the raspberries, dollops of whipped cream and serve immediately. Alternatively, you can serve at room temperature and then garnish, just keep in mind that the soufflés will deflate a bit as they sit but they are still excellent.

Makes 4 portions

Pear & Cranberry Cobbler

Butter for the pie plate
6 cups of peeled and 1/2 inch diced pears
1 cup fresh (or thawed from frozen) cranberries
1/3 cup packed brown sugar
1 tablespoon cornstarch
1 tablespoon lemon juice or lime juice
1/4 teaspoon ground nutmeg
1 cup all-purpose flour
1/2 cup whole wheat flour
2 tablespoons sugar
2 teaspoons baking powder
1 teaspoon baking soda
1/2 teaspoon salt
1/4 cup frozen butter
3/4 cup buttermilk
1 teaspoon chopped lemon zest

1. Preheat oven to 400 degrees Fahrenheit and prepare a 9-inch pie plate by buttering it.
2. Mix the pears, cranberries, brown sugar, cornstarch, lemon or lime juice, and the nutmeg together and spread into the prepared pie plate.
3. In a separate bowl, mix the all-purpose flour, whole wheat flour, sugar, baking powder, baking soda, and salt together. Grate in the frozen butter with a cheese grater and toss in. Add the buttermilk and the lemon zest and mix until just combined. Drop by spoonfuls onto the fruit.
4. Bake for approximately 35 minutes until topping and fruit are cooked. Serve warm with ice cream or whipped cream.

Makes one 9-inch cobbler

Indian Spiced Rice Pudding

"A mildly spiced rice pudding inspired by the flavours of India"

1 cup Basmati rice
2 cups water
Butter, for buttering the baking dish
2 large eggs
1/2 cup sugar
3/4 teaspoon salt
1 cup whipping cream
1 cup milk
1/2 teaspoon ground cinnamon
1/4 teaspoon ground cloves
6 black cardamom pods, slightly broken
1 teaspoon fennel seed
1/2 teaspoon whole black peppercorns
Heavy cream, dried currants, and toasted slivered almonds, for serving

1. Preheat oven to 375 degrees.
2. Combine basmati rice and water in a pot. Bring to a boil. Cover and turn to low heat to simmer for 10 to 12 minutes until rice is cooked.
3. Butter an 8-cup casserole dish equipped with a lid.
4. In a large bowl, combine the eggs, sugar, salt, whipping cream, milk, cinnamon, and cloves. Gradually stir in the hot cooked rice – this must be done slowly to prevent the eggs from turning into scrambled eggs.
5. Pour this mixture into the prepared casserole dish. Place the cardamom pods, fennel seeds, and peppercorns in a piece of cheesecloth and tie tightly: submerse this spice packet into the rice pudding.
6. Bake covered for approximately 40 minutes or until the pudding is almost set in the center. Remove from the oven and let stand covered for approximately 10 to 15 minutes.
7. Stir to evenly distribute spice flavour. Remove spice packet and discard. Serve warm garnished with heavy cream, currants, and toasted almonds.

Makes 8 - 1/2 cup servings

Rum Raisin Bread Pudding

"An easy seasonal recipe instead of a traditional Christmas pudding"

1/2 cup raisins
1/2 cup currants
1/2 packed cup pitted dates, chopped fine
1 cup boiling water
1 – 454g (1 pound) French loaf
Butter for the pan
4 large eggs, beaten
1 cup sugar
1 teaspoon vanilla extract
1 teaspoon ground cinnamon
1/2 teaspoon ground cloves
1/2 teaspoon ground nutmeg
1/2 teaspoon salt
Zest from 2 lemons, finely chopped
1 apple, cored & grated
2 cups 10%MF cream (half and half)
2 cups milk (2%MF or 3.5%Homogenized)
2 tablespoons butter
1 – 300ml can sweetened condensed milk
2 to 3 tablespoons dark rum
Vanilla bean ice cream
Mint leaves, optional

1. Preheat oven to 400 degrees Fahrenheit.
2. Let the raisins, currants, and dates soak in the boiling water for 20 minutes, then drain and set aside.
3. Tear the French bread into approximate 1 inch to 2 inch chunks and spread evenly on a large baking sheet. Bake in the oven for 10 minutes, tossing the pieces around about halfway through. Remove from the oven and set aside.
4. Decrease the oven temperature to 350 degrees and prepare a 9x13 baking dish by buttering it.

5. In a large bowl, combine the eggs, sugar, vanilla, cinnamon, cloves, nutmeg, salt, and the zest thoroughly. Stir in the grated apple and the drained reserved raisins, currants, and dates. Whisk in the cream and milk. Add the reserved toasted bread pieces and toss together thoroughly with your hands. Let sit for 10 minutes for the bread pieces to absorb.

6. Transfer this mixture evenly into the prepared baking dish (and scrape all liquid from the bowl). Dot the surface with small bits of the 2 tbsp butter. Bake for approximately 45 minutes until the top browns and puffs up. Also, an inserted butter knife should come out clean. Let sit for 10 to 15 minutes before cutting.

7. Empty the can of sweetened condensed milk into a pot and heat gently until warm. Remove from the heat and stir in the rum.

8. Plate the bread pudding pieces warm with vanilla bean ice cream, drizzled with rum sauce, and each garnished with a sprig of fresh mint.

Makes 12 portions

Scottish Dundee Cake & Scotch Infused Whip Cream

"A famous traditional Scottish fruit cake with rich flavour and texture"

1.25 cups sultanas
2/3 cup currants
1/2 cup dark raisins
1/4 cup chopped mixed peel*
Zest from 1 lemon, chopped
Zest from 1 large orange, chopped
1/4 cup scotch whiskey*
3/4 cup butter, room temperature
1/3 cup dark brown sugar
1/3 cup white granulated sugar
3 large eggs
1/3 cup milk
1.5 cups flour
1 teaspoon baking powder
2 tablespoons ground almonds
1/2 teaspoon salt
20 whole blanched almonds

1. Preheat oven to 325 degrees. Prepare a 9-inch round cake pan with baking spray (and with parchment paper if desired).
2. Combine sultanas, currants, raisins, peel, zests, and whiskey together in a mixing bowl.
3. In a separate bowl beat the butter with the two sugars, scraping down the sides as necessary. Gradually add each egg and continue beating until fully combined. Add this mixture and the milk to the fruit/whiskey mixture and combine thoroughly.
4. In a separate bowl combine all the dry ingredients: Flour, baking powder, ground almonds, and salt. Add this into the other mixture and fold to combine.
5. Spread mixture evenly into prepared pan and top decoratively with the almonds.

6. Bake for approximately 45 minutes or until a tooth pick inserted comes out clean. Let cool in the pan on a rack for at least 20 minutes. Cut and serve with Scotch infused whip cream.

250ml whipping cream
1 tablespoon white granulated sugar
1 tablespoon scotch whiskey*

1. On high speed beat the cream and the sugar together. When it just starts to get thick, add the whiskey and continue beating until fully whipped.

*Mixed Peel is one of those ingredients that is featured in a lot of British baking, from traditional fruit cakes like Dundee Cake or Christmas Cake to teatime fare like the Hot Cross Buns. Mixed peel is basically candied lemon and orange peel, and it is usually available in the baking aisle of your major grocery store.

*Scotch whiskey – In this recipe I highly recommend using a scotch that's smoky so you can detect the flavour of the scotch in the recipe. In other words, you want to use one that is made with peat smoke. Look for whiskeys from the Islay region of Scotland. One variety that is extremely bold, that has complex smoky peat flavour is the "Laphroaig" brand – very common at most liquor stores.

MUFFINS, LOAVES, & BREADS

Carrot Bran Muffins

1.5 cups whole wheat flour
1.5 cups natural bran
2/3 cup brown sugar
1/4 cup ground flax seed
2 teaspoons baking soda
1.5 teaspoons ground cinnamon
1/2 teaspoon salt
1/4 teaspoon ground cloves
1/4 teaspoon ground nutmeg
1 cup finely grated carrot
2 large eggs
1.5 cups milk
1/4 cup unsweetened apple sauce
1/4 cup canola oil
2 tablespoons lemon juice

1. Preheat oven to 400° F (200 °C) and prepare a 12-cup muffin pan with baking spray.
2. Combine the whole wheat flour, natural bran, brown sugar, ground flax seed, baking soda, cinnamon, salt, cloves, and nutmeg in a mixing bowl.
3. Toss the grated carrot into this dry mixture.
4. Beat the eggs thoroughly in a separate bowl.
5. Add the milk, apple sauce, canola oil, and lemon juice to the beaten eggs. Continue beating until thoroughly combined.
6. Combine the mixtures in the two bowls together until just mixed. Do not over mix.
7. Spoon the batter equally into the prepared muffin pan.
8. Bake for 20 minutes.
9. Cool slightly in the pan before serving.

Makes 12 large muffins

Cheddar Thyme Biscuits

"Great to serve with almost any soup or stew"

2.25 cups flour
1.5 tablespoons baking powder
1 tablespoon sugar
2 teaspoons dried thyme
2 teaspoons salt
3/4 cup grated old cheddar
6 tablespoons frozen butter
3/4 cup sour cream
7 tablespoons milk

1. Preheat the oven to 450 degrees and spray a baking sheet with baking spray or line with parchment paper.
2. In a mixing bowl, combine the flour, baking powder, sugar, thyme, and salt.
3. Toss in the grated cheese to the flour mixture.
4. With a coarse grater, grate the frozen butter into the dry ingredients and gently toss together to mix/coat the butter pieces.
5. In a separate small bowl, stir the sour cream and milk together.
6. Pour the sour cream/milk mixture into the dry ingredients and gently start to mix together until both parts start coming together. Empty the contents onto the counter and work the dough gently until it almost fully comes together and is approximate shape of a 6x8-inch rectangle. Be careful not to overwork the dough, as overworking will make a tough biscuit.
7. With a sharp knife cut the dough into 8 biscuits, place them on the prepared baking sheet and bake for approximately 10-12 minutes until cooked and slightly golden.

Makes 8 portions

Rosemary Parmesan Biscuits

"I highly recommend grating the cheese from a block of Parmigiano-Reggiano"

2.25 cups flour
1.5 tablespoons baking powder
1 tablespoon sugar
1 tablespoon finely chopped fresh rosemary
1.5 teaspoons salt
3/4 cup grated Parmigiano-Reggiano cheese
6 tablespoons frozen butter
3/4 cup sour cream
1/2 cup milk

1. Preheat the oven to 450 degrees and spray a baking sheet with baking spray or line with parchment paper.
2. In a mixing bowl, combine the flour, baking powder, sugar, rosemary, and salt.
3. Toss in the grated cheese to the flour mixture.
4. With a coarse grater, grate the frozen butter into the dry ingredients and gently toss together to mix/coat the butter pieces.
5. In a separate small bowl, stir the sour cream and milk together.
6. Pour the sour cream/milk mixture into the dry ingredients and gently start to mix together until both parts start coming together. Empty the contents onto the counter and work the dough gently until it almost fully comes together and is approximate shape of a 6x8-inch rectangle. **Be careful not to overwork the dough, as overworking will make a tough biscuit.**
7. With a sharp knife cut the dough into 8 biscuits, place them on the prepared baking sheet and bake for approximately 10-12 minutes until cooked and slightly golden.

Makes 8 portions

Holiday Cranberry Buttermilk Scones

"Whether for breakfast or with an afternoon coffee, these scones filled with cranberries and warm spices offer up an unforgettable treat"

1 cup whole wheat flour
1 cup   all-purpose flour
1/2 cup white sugar
2 teaspoons baking powder
2 teaspoons baking soda
1.5 teaspoons ground cinnamon
1/2 teaspoon salt
1/4 teaspoon ground cloves
1/4 teaspoon ground nutmeg
1/2 cup butter, cold or frozen
1/2 cup frozen cranberries, halved or coarsely chopped
1 cup buttermilk
1.5 tablespoons buttermilk
2 tablespoons icing sugar
1/2 teaspoon ground cinnamon

1. Preheat oven to 425° F (220 °C) and prepare a baking sheet with baking spray or line it with parchment paper.
2. Combine the whole wheat flour, all purpose flour, sugar, baking powder, baking soda, the 1.5 teaspoons cinnamon, salt, cloves, and nutmeg together in a mixing bowl.
3. Grate the butter into the dry mixture with a coarse size grater. Stop at intervals to lightly toss the butter particles into the flour mixture to keep the butter from lumping together.
4. Add the cranberries and toss into this mixture.
5. Mix in the 1 cup of buttermilk until the mixture is just starting to combine. Turn out onto countertop and knead until the dough just comes together and forms a smooth ball. DO NOT OVERMIX. Lightly flour the surface of the dough and gently press into a flat round disc approximately 3/4 inch (2cm) thick. Transfer the dough to the prepared baking sheet.
6. Brush the 1.5 tablespoons of buttermilk over the surface of the dough.

7. Mix the 2 tablespoons of icing sugar with the 1/2 teaspoon of cinnamon and evenly sprinkle this mix over the surface of the dough.
8. Cut the dough into 8 equal pie shaped sections, but do not separate them – keep the disc in one large circle. This will help support the sides of each portion as they rise in the oven.
9. Bake for 20 minutes until golden brown.
10. Let cool slightly, and then cut the sections to separate and serve immediately with butter, if desired.

Makes 8 scones

Lower Calorie Pumpkin Cupcakes

"This recipe is from my time working with Splenda Canada. By using Splenda brand no calorie sweetener, we can cut out a lot of the calories from cupcakes. Although the recipe still has 1/2 cup of oil (for moisture/richness), these are still healthier (with the addition of pumpkin) and lower calories than normal cupcakes."

1 & 1/2 cups whole wheat flour
1/2 cup SPLENDA® No Calorie Sweetener, Granulated
1 teaspoon baking powder
1 teaspoon baking soda
1 teaspoon ground cinnamon
1/2 teaspoon salt
1/2 teaspoon ground nutmeg
1/4 teaspoon ground cloves
1 large egg
1 & 3/4 cups canned pumpkin
1/2 cup canola oil

Icing Ingredients
1 – 250g package spreadable low fat cream cheese
1/2 cup SPLENDA® No Calorie Sweetener, Granulated
1 teaspoon vanilla extract

1. Preheat oven to 400 degrees Fahrenheit and prepare a 12-cup muffin pan with baking spray.
2. Combine the whole wheat flour, SPLENDA® No Calorie Sweetener Granulated, baking powder, baking soda, ground cinnamon, salt, ground nutmeg, and ground cloves in a mixing bowl.
3. Beat the egg thoroughly in a separate bowl.
4. Add the canned pumpkin and canola oil to the beaten egg. Mix until thoroughly combined.
5. Combine the mixtures in the two bowls together until just mixed. Do not over mix. The batter will be a bit stiffer than a typical cupcake or muffin batter.
6. Spoon the batter equally into the prepared muffin pan, taking the time to evenly smooth the batter in each cup.
7. Bake for approximately 18 to 20 minutes.

8. Remove from the pan and cool completely on a wire rack.
9. Combine the cream cheese, SPLENDA® No Calorie Sweetener Granulated, and vanilla to form an icing.
10. Spread the icing equally over the tops of the thoroughly cooled cupcakes.

Makes 12 cupcakes

No Knead Cinnamon Raisin Bread

"This bread recipe requires no kneading and produces a wonderful crusty loaf. Lots of time and a cast iron pot is the secret. Serve warm with butter and a generous sprinkle of more cinnamon and sugar."

3 cups all-purpose flour
1/2 cup raisins
1/4 cup wheat germ
1.5 tablespoons cinnamon
1.5 teaspoons salt
1/2 teaspoon instant yeast
1.75 cups slightly warm water
More flour for dusting

1. In a large bowl, or a plastic container, mix together the 3 cups flour, raisins, wheat germ, cinnamon, salt, and yeast. Stir in the water until thoroughly mixed. Seal the bowl with plastic wrap (or seal with lid on the container) and let stand at room temperature for 12 to 24 hours.
2. After the 12 to 24 hours, dust half of a cotton towel very liberally with flour. Dust the counter liberally with flour. With your flour dusted hands, scrape the wet dough onto the counter and fold it over on itself once or twice, while gently and quickly shaping it into a ball. Transfer the dough seam side down to the flour dusted section of the towel. Liberally dust the top of the dough and fold the towel over the dough to rest. Rest the dough during the next step.
3. Place a medium to large cast iron pot and the lid (an enamel coated cast iron pot and lid works great too) in your oven and preheat to 450 degrees Fahrenheit (425 degrees if convection).
4. Once your oven is at the required temperature, carefully remove the preheated pot. Remove the heated lid. Unfold the towel off the dough. Place your hand gently under the dough by sliding your hand under the towel and turn dough over into the pot (seam side up). Remove the towel. Don't fuss with the dough. Place the heated lid back onto the pot and place back in the oven. Bake for 30 minutes with lid on. Then remove the lid and bake another 15 minutes until loaf is browned.

5. Carefully place the cooked loaf onto a cooling rack and let sit at least 15 to 20 minutes before slicing. Use a good bread knife as outer crust will be wonderfully crunchy.

Makes 1 loaf

No Knead Rustic Rye Bread

"This bread recipe requires no kneading and produces a wonderful crusty loaf. Lots of time and a cast iron pot is the secret. Although denser than a regular no knead bread, it's a wonderful loaf reminiscent of a bread you would imagine coming from a rustic farmhouse. Serve warm with butter and honey – that's how our family prefers it!"

1.5 cups all-purpose flour
1 cup rye flour
1/2 cup wheat germ
1.5 teaspoons sugar
1.5 teaspoons salt
1/4 teaspoon instant yeast
1.5 cups & 2 tablespoons slightly warm water
More all-purpose flour for dusting

1. In a large bowl, or a plastic container, mix together the 1.5 cups all-purpose flour, rye flour, wheat germ, sugar, salt, and yeast. Stir in the water until thoroughly mixed. Seal the bowl with plastic wrap (or seal with lid on the container) and let stand at room temperature for 24 hours. Because it's denser than a regular white loaf it won't rise as much so it needs the full 24 hours.
2. After the 24 hours, dust half of a cotton towel very liberally with flour. Dust the counter liberally with flour. With your flour dusted hands, scrape the wet dough onto the counter and fold it over on itself once or twice, while gently and quickly shaping it into a ball. Transfer the dough seam side down to the flour dusted section of the towel. Liberally dust the top of the dough and fold the towel over the dough to rest. Rest the dough during the next step.
3. Place a medium to large cast iron pot and the lid (an enamel coated cast iron pot and lid works great too) in your oven and preheat to 450 degrees Fahrenheit (425 degrees if convection).
4. Once your oven is at the required temperature, carefully remove the preheated pot. Remove the heated lid. Unfold the towel off the dough. Place your hand gently under the dough by sliding your hand under the towel and turn dough over into the pot (seam side up). Remove the towel. Don't fuss with the dough. Place the heated lid back onto the

pot and place back in the oven. Bake for 30 minutes with lid on. Then remove the lid and bake another 15 minutes until loaf is browned.

5. Carefully place the cooked loaf onto a cooling rack and let sit at least 15 to 20 minutes before slicing. Use a good bread knife as outer crust will be wonderfully crunchy.

Makes 1 loaf

RECIPE NOTES

No Knead Sourdough Bread

"This bread recipe requires no kneading and produces a wonderful crusty loaf. A cast iron pot is the secret. You'll be 8 days from the time you begin your starter to the time you bake your loaves, but you will love the results! Break out the kitchen scale and buy some distilled water for this recipe (tap water won't work)."

For the starter:
200g of all-purpose flour
200ml of distilled water, room temperature

For 2 loaves of bread:
5 cups all-purpose flour
1 cup prepared sourdough starter
3 teaspoons sugar
3 teaspoons salt
1/2 teaspoon instant yeast
2 cups + 4 tablespoons distilled water, room temperature
More all-purpose flour for dusting

1. Begin the starter by combining 100g of the flour with 100ml of the water in a medium glass bowl. Cover the bowl loosely with plastic wrap or a cotton towel to let the dough breathe and let sit at room temperature for 24 hours. Then for each of the five days afterwards add 20g of flour and 20ml (4 teaspoons) of water each day, while stirring to combine and recovering with the towel and letting stand at room temperature for 24 hours after each addition.
2. To recap the starter procedure: Day 1 begin the starter; Day 2 feed the starter; Day 3 feed the starter; Day 4 feed the starter; Day 5 feed the starter; Day 6 feed the starter; Day 7 the starter is ready for the next step.
3. On Day 7, in two separate large bowls or two plastic containers, mix together the following ingredients in EACH of the containers: 2.5 cups all-purpose flour, 1/2 cup of the prepared starter, 1.5 teaspoons sugar, 1.5 teaspoons salt, and 1/4 teaspoon yeast. In EACH container stir in the 1 cup + 2 tablespoons water until thoroughly mixed. It will be a

wet dough. Seal the bowl with plastic wrap (or seal with lid on the container) and let stand at room temperature for 24 hours.

4. On Day 8, dust half of two cotton towels very liberally with flour. Dust the counter liberally with flour. With your flour dusted hands, scrape the two wet doughs onto the counter separately and fold each of them over on itself once or twice, while gently and quickly shaping them into balls. Transfer the doughs seam side down to the flour dusted sections of the towels. Liberally dust the top of the doughs and fold the towels over the doughs to rest. Rest the doughs during the next step.

5. Place 2 medium to large cast iron pots and the lids (enamel coated cast iron pots and lids work great too) in your oven and preheat to 450 degrees Fahrenheit (425 degrees if convection).

6. Once your oven is at the required temperature, carefully remove the preheated pots. Remove the heated lids. Unfold the towels off the doughs. Place your hand gently under each of the doughs by sliding your hand under the towel and turn dough over into each of the pots (seam side up). Remove the towels. Don't fuss with the doughs. Place the heated lids back onto the pots and place back in the oven. Bake for 30 minutes with lids on. Then remove the lids and bake another 15 minutes until loaves are browned.

7. Carefully place the cooked loaves onto a cooling rack and let sit at least 15 to 20 minutes before slicing. Use a good bread knife as outer crust will be wonderfully crunchy.

Makes 2 loaves

MISCELLANEOUS

Curry Powder Blend

"There is something wonderful about creating your own spice blends. This is my personal favourite for curry. Use it whenever a recipe calls for curry powder."

6 black cardamom pods
1/2 cup coriander seeds
1/3 cup cumin seeds
2 tablespoons fenugreek seeds
2 tablespoons fennel seeds
1 tablespoon black peppercorns
1 tablespoon yellow mustard seeds
1 tablespoon brown mustard seeds
3 tablespoons ground turmeric

1. Crack open the cardamom pods by pressing the pods on a cutting board with the side of knife. Empty the contents of the pods into a frying pan and discard the pod shells.
2. Add the coriander, cumin, fenugreek, fennel, peppercorns, and both mustard seeds to the pan. Stir to combine. Heat the pan over medium-high heat and cook until the ingredients start smoking a bit and crackling a bit while shaking/stirring the ingredients almost constantly. Be careful not to burn them. Immediately transfer the ingredients to a stainless steel or glass bowl to stop the cooking process. Let sit until the ingredients have fully come to room temperature.
3. Grind in a spice grinder in batches until the whole amount has been ground to a powder. Stir in the turmeric thoroughly and store in an airtight container.

Makes 1.5 cups

Cheese Soufflés with Creamy Leek Sauce

"Soufflés are not as difficult as some people think, and this makes a wonderful treat. Baking time will depend on the temperature of your raw eggs. The finished soufflés will deflate a bit as they sit, but this is normal."

Butter for ramekins
1/3 cup finely ground parmesan cheese
3 tablespoons butter
3 tablespoons flour
1 teaspoon Dijon mustard
3/4 teaspoon salt
1/4 teaspoon ground cayenne pepper
1 cup milk
100g grated aged cheddar cheese
6 large eggs, yolks separated from whites
1 teaspoon sugar
<u>Creamy leek Sauce</u>
2 tablespoons butter
1 leek, white part only, halved and sliced thin, about 1 cup packed
1 cup whipping cream
3/4 teaspoon salt
1/4 teaspoon pepper

1. Preheat oven to 375 degrees Fahrenheit.
2. Prepare five 1-cup sized (250ml) oven safe ramekins by buttering them and then dusting them with the finely ground parmesan thoroughly; tapping out any excess. After coating all five ramekins, if there is any parmesan left, add it to the grated cheddar.
3. Melt the 3 tablespoons of butter in a medium pot over medium heat. Stir in the flour and reduce the heat to medium/low. Cook for about 2 to 3 minutes to remove the starchy taste of the flour, stirring occasionally.
4. Stir in the mustard, 3/4 teaspoon salt, and cayenne. Slowly whisk in the milk to ensure no lumps, until fully combined. Turn the heat to medium and wait until the mixture just starts to boil to thicken a bit, stirring occasionally.

5. Take the pot off the heat and stir in the grated cheddar until fully melted and combined.

6. Transfer this milk/cheese mixture to a large mixing bowl and let stand for 5 minutes to cool a bit. Then stir in the egg yolks, one at a time, to this mixture.

7. Beat the egg whites in a stand mixture with whisk attachment until foamy, then add the 1 teaspoon of sugar. With the sugar added, beat the egg whites on high speed until stiff peaks form. Stir approximately 1/3 of these whipped egg whites into the cheese mixture. Gently fold in the remaining egg whites thoroughly.

8. Pour the soufflé mixture equally into the prepared ramekins. Once filled, tap them on the counter a few times to knock out any air bubbles. Place the filled ramekins on a baking sheet and bake in the oven for approximately 17 to 20 minutes (depending on the temperature of your eggs), until puffed up, set and cracked on top.

9. While the soufflés are baking, prepare the leek sauce: Melt 2 tablespoons of butter in a medium pan over medium heat. Add the sliced leeks and cook, stirring occasionally, until soft, about 2 to 3 minutes. Stir in the whipping cream and season with the salt and pepper. Then bring to a boil, and then reduce until thickened a bit, about 2 minutes. Remove from heat.

10. Put each hot ramekin on a serving plate and top with equal amounts of the leek sauce. Alternatively, you can let them cool a bit and then garnish with the sauce to serve, just keep in mind that the soufflés will deflate a bit as they sit but they are still excellent.

Makes 5 portions

Cinnamon Nutmeg Milk

"My son Noah created this recipe – he loves it!"

1.5 cups milk
2 tablespoons sugar
1/8 teaspoon salt
1/2 teaspoon ground cinnamon
1/2 teaspoon ground nutmeg
1/4 teaspoon vanilla extract

1. Add all the ingredients to a blender and blend for 2 minutes until the sugar has dissolved.
2. Pour over ice end enjoy.

Makes 1 large drink or 2 smaller ones

Eggs Benedict with Bacon

"Egg yolks and mustard are the emulsifiers that keep this Hollandaise sauce from separating; Egg whites do not play a part in this."

4 large eggs, poached
2 English muffins, split, toasted, & buttered
6 slices bacon, cooked
3 egg yolks
1 tbsp fresh lemon juice
1/2 teaspoon Dijon mustard
2 dashes of hot sauce (like Tabasco brand)
Pinch of salt & pepper
1/2 cup of melted butter
Paprika for garnish

1. Poach the eggs to desired doneness, toast and butter the split muffins, and assemble as follows: per serving place one prepared muffin half, 1.5 slices bacon, & one egg.

2. Put the egg yolks in a blender along with the lemon juice, mustard, hot sauce, salt, and pepper. Puree until fully combined. With the blender running on medium to medium/high speed, slowly drizzle the warm melted butter into the egg yolk mixture until fully combined. Top the prepared eggs/muffins with the Hollandaise sauce. Sprinkle with paprika and serve immediately.

Makes four single egg portions

German Peppernut Cookies (Pfeffernusse)
Recipe from Chef Dez's Mom

1 cup lard (Crisco is recommended)
1 cup milk
2 cups white sugar
2 cups corn syrup
8 1/2 cups flour
2 teaspoons peppermint extract
1 1/2 teaspoons baking powder
1 teaspoon ground black pepper
1 teaspoon ground nutmeg
1 teaspoon ground cinnamon
Icing sugar

1. Heat together the lard, milk, sugar, and corn syrup. Mix well, and let cool. Preheat oven to 350 degrees.
2. Add the flour, peppermint extract, baking powder, pepper, nutmeg, and cinnamon, and mix well.
3. Roll into small balls (about the size of walnuts) and bake for 15 minutes.
4. Shake hot cookies in a bag of icing sugar to coat.

Jack O' Lantern Devilled Eggs – Makes 12 halves

"Time to have a little fun with your eggs this Halloween! Don't fuss too much with these as each one should be unique. Adding a little butter to the egg yolk mixture helps the filling hold up better."

6 large hard-boiled eggs, peeled
Paprika for sprinkling
2 tablespoons mayonnaise
1 tablespoon room temperature butter
1 tablespoon Dijon mustard
1 tablespoon sweet green relish
2 teaspoons red wine vinegar
1/2 teaspoon sugar
1/4 teaspoon Worcestershire sauce
1/4 teaspoon salt
1/8 teaspoon pepper
Skin from 1 cucumber

1. Carefully cut the eggs in half lengthwise. Remove the yolks and place them in a small mixing bowl.
2. Sprinkle some paprika over the cut side of the egg whites.
3. To the reserved egg yolks, and the mayonnaise, butter, mustard, relish, vinegar, sugar, Worcestershire, salt and pepper. Mash until smooth. Spoon this mixture into a disposable sandwich bag and then cut the corner off to make a piping bag. Carefully pipe this mixture equally into the hollowed egg whites. Chill in the refrigerator during the next step.
4. Using a vegetable peeler, take long strips of skin off a cucumber. Cut the dark green skin strips into many small triangles to decorate as the eyes and noses. Use a small round cookie cutter (a fluted edge one works best) to make semi-circle shapes to decorate as mouths. Decorate the filling in the egg whites with the cucumber skin eyes, noses, and mouths (the pointed tip of a small knife will be helpful in carefully placing the face decorations, or a sanitized pair of tweezers).
5. Arrange on a platter and serve immediately or refrigerate until needed.

Marinated & Grilled Portobellos

"Who would have ever thought that a mushroom could have this much flavour!"

1/4 cup olive oil
1/4 cup balsamic vinegar
2 teaspoons dried oregano leaves
1 teaspoon dried basil leaves
1 teaspoon sugar
1/2 teaspoon salt
1/4 teaspoon fresh cracked pepper
2 large portobello mushrooms

1. Whisk all the ingredients (except for the mushrooms) together in a small bowl.
2. Place the mushrooms and marinade in a plastic bag, ensuring it is sealed.
3. Gently handle the bag back and forth to coat the mushrooms.
4. Marinate in the refrigerator for 2 to 24 hours. Flip the bag once or twice during this time period to allow for more even flavour saturation.
5. Remove the mushrooms from the marinade and grill them on a hot barbeque until slightly charred and cooked through, approximately 3 – 5 minutes per side.

Serves 2

Serving Suggestions:

- Use in place of a hamburger patties. Serve on buns with a variety of toppings like roasted garlic mayonnaise, melted cheese, lettuce, tomato, etc.
- Turn your ordinary eggs benedict into something completely different. Use one of these portobellos as a replacement for the English muffin for a low carb experience.
- Slice them and use to top a variety of dishes like steaks & salads or add to pasta dishes.

Horseradish Butter

"Great on grilled steaks!"

1/2 cup salted butter, room temperature
2 Tbsp jarred horseradish
2 Tbsp minced green onions
Season to taste with salt & pepper

Mix all ingredients together and store at room temperature for same day use, or in the refrigerator for future use.

Makes approximately 3/4 cup

Marinated Olives

2 cups drained kalamata olives
2 cups drained green olives
1 cup extra virgin olive oil
5 anchovy filets, chopped fine
1/4 cup chopped fresh rosemary
1/4 cup chopped fresh thyme
1/4 cup fresh lemon juice, zest reserved
2 tablespoons minced onion
2 tablespoons minced garlic
2 tablespoons fennel seeds
1 teaspoon fresh cracked pepper
Finely minced lemon zest from above
3 tablespoons balsamic vinegar

1. Combine and mix all of the ingredients except for the balsamic. Cover and chill for 8 hours or up to 3 days.
2. Bring to room temperature. Remove with a slotted spoon and stir in the balsamic vinegar.

Preserved Lemons – makes 40 wedges

"It will be 1 month before they're ready, but they will last indefinitely in the refrigerator. Use in any application that you would lemons, or just to brighten up a soup, stew, sauce, salad, etc. When they're ready just rinse, and then chop with the whole skin (zest and pith)."

5 lemons
Large Mason Jar
8 teaspoons kosher salt

1. Trim the ends of the lemons and cut each lemon into 8 equal wedges, removing the seeds where possible.
2. Start filling the Mason Jar alternating with layers of lemon wedges and salt, until all the wedges and salt are in the jar. Top with any remaining juices from cutting the lemons. You may have to press the wedges in a bit if you are using large lemons.
3. Screw the lid on the jar. Shake and rotate the jar until most of the salt has come off the side of the jar.
4. Store in the refrigerator for 1 month while flipping over the jar every 5 days.
5. To use some of the lemon in a recipe, rinse with water and chop (skin and all).

Roasted Pumpkin Seeds – makes 1.5 cups

1.5 cups raw pumpkin seeds, rinsed and patted dry
2 tablespoons canola oil
2 – 2.5 teaspoons seasoning salt (see recipe in this chapter)

1. Preheat oven to 450 degrees.
2. Toss the seeds with the oil and seasoning salt and scatter them on a baking sheet large enough so that they are a single layer.
3. Bake for approximately 10 to 20 minutes (depending on their size) until golden brown, tossing them around every 5 minute interval.
4. Let cool on the baking sheet to crisp up further. Serve them at room temperature.

Individual Monte Cristo Bread Pudding – makes 1 portion

"The classic Monte Cristo Sandwich, but prepared like a bread pudding in an individual baking dish. By preparing this the night before, it makes for a quick gourmet breakfast in the morning."

2 thick slices of sandwich bread
50g ham, diced small
40g Gruyere or Gouda cheese, grated
1 large egg
1/3 cup milk
1 tablespoon finely chopped onion
1/4 teaspoon Worcestershire sauce
1/8 teaspoon dry mustard
1/8 teaspoon salt
Pinch of pepper
1 to 2 drops Tabasco brand sauce
Finely chopped fresh parsley for garnish, optional

1. Cube 1 slice of the bread into approximately 1/2 inch cubes and place them in the bottom of a 2-cup oven-proof dish.
2. Top with the ham, 20g of cheese, and the second slice of bread, cubed.
3. In a small bowl, mix thoroughly together the egg, milk, onion, Worcestershire, mustard, salt, pepper, and Tabasco, and pour over the bread, ham, and cheese in the dish.
4. Top with the second 20g of grated cheese. Cover with plastic wrap and refrigerate overnight for the bread to soak up the egg mixture.
5. Preheat oven to 350 degrees.
6. Remove the plastic wrap and bake uncovered for approximately 35 to 45 minutes until the egg has cooked through and the cheese has browned. Let stand for 5 minutes, garnish with parsley and serve.

*Helpful Tip: If mixing the egg mixture for more than one recipe (one portion) do not add the onion to the egg mixture. Instead add the 1 tbsp chopped onion directly onto the top layer of cubed bread for each portion and pour the egg mixture over top. This will ensure that each portion gets the right amount of onion.

Monte Cristo Breakfast Casserole

"The classic Monte Cristo Sandwich, but prepared in a breakfast casserole format"

12 slices of sandwich bread
300g ham slices
300g Swiss or Emmentaler cheese, grated
1/3 cup finely chopped onion
6 eggs, beaten
2 cups milk
2 teaspoons Worcestershire sauce
1 teaspoon dry mustard
1 teaspoon salt
8 to 16 drops Tabasco sauce
1/2 teaspoon pepper
Finely chopped fresh parsley for garnish, optional

1. Prepare a 9x13 oven safe dish with baking spray or butter.
2. Arrange 6 slices of the bread in the oven safe dish.
3. Top evenly with the ham, then 200g of the cheese, the chopped onion, and the next 6 slices of bread.
4. In a bowl, mix thoroughly together the eggs, milk, Worcestershire, mustard, salt, and Tabasco. Pour this mixture over the bread, ham, and cheese in the dish, and then sprinkle evenly with the pepper.
5. Top with the remaining 100g of grated cheese. Cover and refrigerate for at least one hour, up to 12 hours, for the bread to soak up the egg mixture.
6. Preheat oven to 350 degrees.
7. Remove the cover from the dish and bake uncovered for approximately 35 to 40 minutes until the egg has cooked through and the top has browned. Let stand for 5 minutes, garnish with parsley if desired and serve.

Makes 6 portions

Scotch Eggs

"A classic and popular Scottish appetizer... or great as a snack or breakfast too!"

1 cup soda cracker crumbs
1/2 cup minced fresh parsley
6 large hard-boiled eggs
680g (1.5 pounds) pork breakfast sausages

1. Preheat oven to 375 degrees
2. Mix the cracker crumbs and the parsley together in a shallow dish.
3. Peel the eggs. Squeeze the sausage meat from the casings and discard the casings. Encase each of the peeled eggs in an equal amount of the sausage meat.
4. Roll each of the sausage coated eggs in the crumb/parsley mixture. Place on a baking sheet and bake for 30-35 minutes until the sausage meat is cooked through, turning occasionally.
5. Store in refrigerator until ready to serve. Cut each egg into 4 wedges for serving.

Makes 24 wedges

Seasoning Salt

"Never buy store bought seasoning salt again – make your own!"

1/2 cup salt
3 tablespoons coarse grind pepper
2 tablespoons smoked paprika
1/2 tablespoon onion powder
1/2 tablespoon garlic powder

1. Mix all ingredients together and store indefinitely.

Taco Seasoning

"Why buy store-bought, when you can make it yourself? Taco Tuesday will never be the same again!"

2 tablespoons chili powder
5 teaspoons smoked paprika
4.5 teaspoons ground cumin
3 teaspoons onion powder
2.5 teaspoons garlic powder
1.5 teaspoons salt
1/8 to 1/4 teaspoon ground cayenne pepper

1. Mix all ingredients together and store indefinitely.

Swedish Cabbage Rolls

"This is a recipe that I perfected for a good client of mine. She came to me with a family recipe and wanted me to make it better."

8 large green cabbage leaves
227g (1/2 pound) lean ground beef
227g (1/2 pound) lean ground pork
3/4 cup cooked rice
2/3 cup milk
1/4 cup finely chopped onion
1 large egg
1 clove garlic, finely chopped
1.5 teaspoons salt
1 teaspoon Worcestershire sauce
1/4 teaspoon sambal oelek, optional*
1/4 teaspoon pepper

Sauce Ingredients
1 – 398ml can of diced tomatoes, drained well
1 – 284ml can of condensed tomato soup
2 tablespoons minced onion
1 tablespoon dark brown sugar
1 tablespoon Worcestershire sauce
1 tablespoon cornstarch

More salt & pepper
1 tablespoon cold butter, broken into small bits
Sour cream, for serving

1. Carefully remove the eight leaves from the cabbage without breaking them by first coring out the bottom of the cabbage as much as possible. Cut out the thickest center part of the rib of each leaf – approximately 1 to 2 inches worth. Steam the leaves over boiling water for approximately 4 minutes until soft. Set the leaves aside to drain in a colander.
2. Preheat the oven to 350 degrees.

3. In a bowl, thoroughly combine the beef, pork, rice, milk, onion, egg, garlic, salt, Worcestershire, sambal oelek and pepper together. Score the top of the mixture to mark 8 equal portions of this mixture.

4. Put one portion in each of the cabbage leaves. Roll up the sides of the leaf around the meat mixture and roll up towards the bottom part of the leaf where the rib was cut out. Repeat with the other 7 leaves and place them tightly together in a 9 x 9 size casserole dish.

5. Mix the sauce ingredients together and pour evenly over the cabbage rolls. Sprinkle with salt, pepper and the small bits of butter. Bake for 1 hour, and then let sit for 15-20 minutes before serving with dollops of sour cream.

Makes 8 large cabbage rolls

*Sambal oelek is an Indonesian chili sauce or paste typically made from a mixture of a variety of chili peppers. One can usually find it down the imported (or Asian) food aisle of major grocery stores.

INDEX

ABOUT THE AUTHOR

Chef Dez (Gordon Desormeaux) resides in the Fraser Valley of British Columbia, Canada with his family. His passion for food and people is second to none and anyone who has attended his live performances would agree.

Thousands of have rekindled their romance for the culinary arts because of his infectious enthusiasm for bringing ingredients together.

www.chefdez.com

Manufactured by Amazon.ca
Bolton, ON